another 100
of the world's best
houses

another 100
of the world's best
houses

another 100

of the world's best

houses

images
Publishing

Fifth reprint 2005
The Images Publishing Group Reference Number: 634
Fourth reprint 2005
The Images Publishing Group Reference Number: 609
Third reprint 2004
The Images Publishing Group Reference Number: 601
Second reprint 2004
The Images Publishing Group Reference Number: 585
First reprinted 2004
The Images Publishing Group Reference Number: 523

First published in Australia in 2003 by
The Images Publishing Group Pty Ltd
ABN 89 059 734 431
6 Bastow Place, Mulgrave, Victoria, 3170, Australia
Telephone: +61 3 9561 5544 Facsimile: +61 3 9561 4860
books@images.com.au
www.imagespublishing.com
The Images Publishing Group Reference Number: 520

National Library of Australia Cataloguing-in-Publication data

Another 100 of the World's Best Houses.

ISBN: 1 920744 24 X
Includes Index.

1 Architecture, Domestic – Pictorial Works. 2 Architecture, Domestic.

328

Coordinating Editor: Robyn Beaver

Designed by The Graphic Image Studio Pty Ltd, Mulgrave, Australia
www.tgis.com.au

Reprinted by Paramount Printing Co. Ltd. in Hong Kong/China

IMAGES has included on its website a page for special notices in relation to this and its
other publications. Please visit www.imagespublishing.com.

Contents

20–22 DALEHAM MEWS

London, UK

bere:architects

Opposite:
Interior view of glass and steel studio

2   Approach to studio from top of staircase

3   Curved glass and steel rooftop studio bathed
    in sunlight, with rooftop planting beyond

Photography: Peter Cook/VIEW

3   2

4

5

6

4 View of gracefully curving polished plaster staircase – a 'coup de theatre'

5 20–22 Daleham Mews, Belsize Park from the houses opposite

6 View of master bedroom

7 View of living room

8 View from dining room toward kitchen, with dramatic rooftop lighting

Photography: Peter Cook/VIEW

7

8

3 ABERDEEN LANE

London, UK

Azman Owens Architects

1

2

Opposite:
Openable timber shutters offer a degree of privacy

2 Concrete walls border the site, allowing privacy

3 View through courtyard door bordering the lane, an intriguing mix of solid and transparent

4 Den, kitchen and living room all face courtyard through big panes of glass

Photography: Keith Collie

3

4

6

5

5 Full-height cupboards to entrance hall double as kitchen cupboards, creating one of the characteristics of the house where all internal separating walls are either insitu concrete or full-height joinery pieces

6 A 'wall' of books faces first floor mezzanine/landing; openable skylight above stair brings natural light into heart of the house

7 Section

8 External concrete wall to master bathroom has a timber-clad 'Japanese' tub and shower, providing a dramatic backdrop

9 Stair has cantilevered concrete treads and a glass balustrade bolted to ends of treads

Photography: Keith Collie

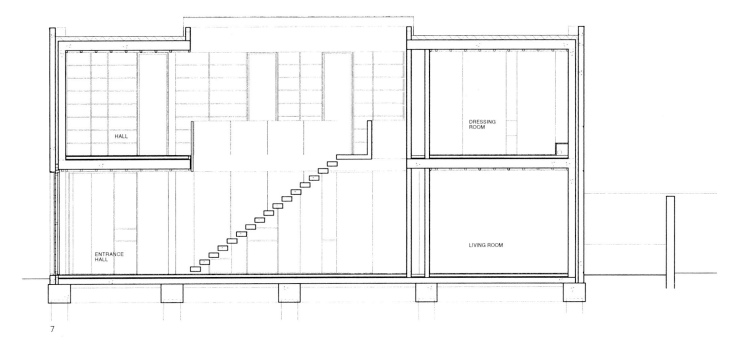

7

DRESSING ROOM

HALL

LIVING ROOM

ENTRANCE HALL

8

9

511 HOUSE

Pacific Palisades, California, USA

Kanner Architects

2

3

4

5

6

7

5 Rear of house at twilight

6 View of two-story living room

7 Kitchen

8 First floor plan

9 View from street at twilight

Photography: John Ellis (5); John Linden Photographer (6,7,9)

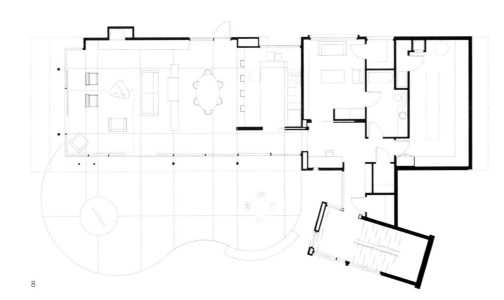

8

9

A CABIN IN THE WOODS

Scientists Cliffs, Maryland, USA

Good Architecture

2

Opposite:
View from woods

2 View from road at twilight

3 Entry hall

4 Living room

Photography: Celia Pearson

3

4

A HOUSE IN THE COUNTRY

Aconcagua Valley, Chile

Germán del Sol, Architect

1   The house is raised above ground level

2&3   Wooden walkways invite outdoor exploration

4   Floor plan

5   Common family living areas flow through house

6   Kitchen is part of the continuous flowing space

7   Vast nature of bathroom relates to the country outside

Photography: Guy St. Claire

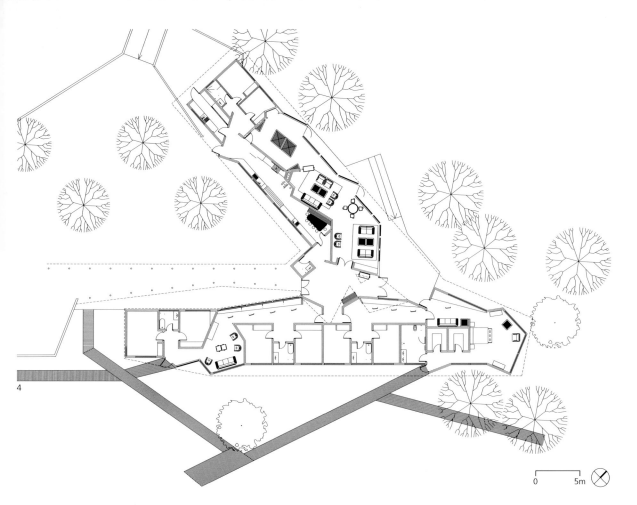

4

5

6

7

ANDREW ROAD HOUSE

Singapore

SCDA Architects Pte Ltd

2

3

4

Opposite:
　Twilight view looking back toward entry
　pavilion and master suite

2　Master bathroom suite, floors and walls in
　volax marble

3　View from master bedroom suite looking
　toward underground parking and entry
　pavilion

4　View of living room looking toward garden,
　floors are silver travertine slabs

Photography: Albert Lim

5

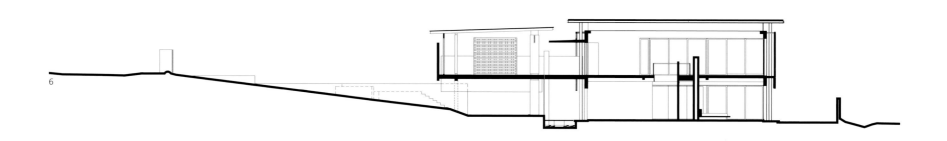

6

5 Front view of house from garden showing cantilevered guest bedroom
6 Section
7 Entry is through granite slabs across 6-inch-deep reflective pool
8 View from entry reflective pool toward main swimming pool
9 View of main swimming pool with infinity edge

Photography: Albert Lim

7

8

9

BERTY HOUSE

East Hampton, New York, USA

Alfredo De Vido Associates

2

3

Opposite:
Front at night

2 Rear garden

3 Bridges

4 Decks

Photography: Norman McGrath

4

5

6

5   Roof structure

6   Family room

7&8   Living room

Photography: Norman McGrath

7

BRICK BAY PAVILION

Brick Bay, Warkworth, New Zealand

Noel Lane Architects

1

2

3

1 Exterior view at night
2 Exterior view looking southeast over Hauraki Gulf
3 Interior view of kitchen/living area, looking over tennis court
4 Bathroom
5 Interior view facing south at night

Photography: Mark Klever

4

5

BURRAWORRIN RESIDENCE

Flinders, Victoria, Australia

Gregory Burgess Architects

2

3

4

5

6 First floor plan

7 Ground floor plan

8 Vestibule stair to lookout

9 View of bar and dining room

10 View of living room looking toward family
   room and dining room

Photography: Trevor Mein

8

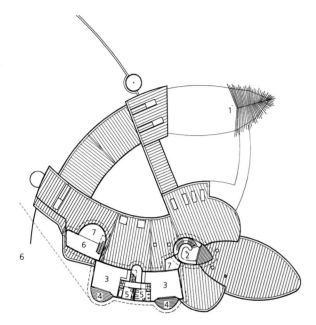

6

1 Canopy
2 Lookout
3 Master bedroom
4 Balcony
5 Bathroom
6 Loft
7 Void

9

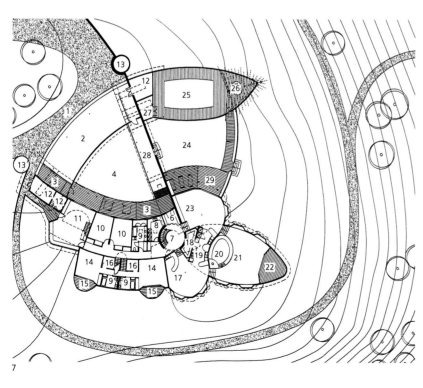

7

1 Driveway
2 Carport
3 Ramp
4 Courtyard
5 Veranda
6 Entry
7 Vestibule
8 Laundry
9 Bathroom
10 Bedroom
11 Rumpus
12 Store
13 Rainwater tank
14 Master bedroom
15 Balcony
16 Alcove
17 Dining
18 Pantry
19 Kitchen
20 Firepit
21 Living
22 Deck
23 Breakfast
24 Terrace
25 Pool
26 Spa
27 Pool equipment
28 Walkway
29 Barbeque

0   10m

10

CANAL HOUSE

Venice, California, USA

Sander Architects

2

3

Opposite:

Canal elevation of main residence

2 Street view of studio with translucent panel walls and steel shade fins

3 Dining and kitchen areas

4 Main residence, ground floor; cross-bracing is both structural and spatial

Photography: Sharon Risedorph

4

5

6

7

5 Master bathroom with custom resin sinks

6 Curved, warped, horizontally sanded
   translucent acrylic panels wrap the atrium

7 Master bedroom, wrapped atrium

8 Atrium with acrylic panels

Photography: Sharon Risedorph

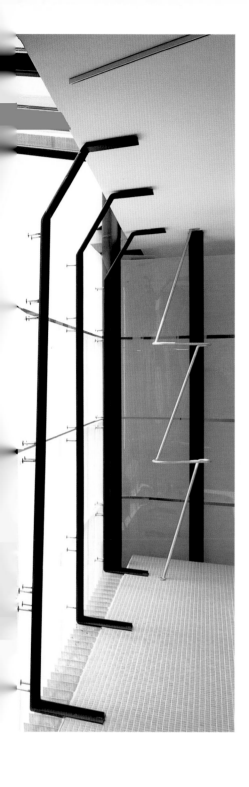

8

CASA DEL SOL FERNÁNDEZ

La Dehesa, Santiago, Chile

Germán del Sol, Architect

1

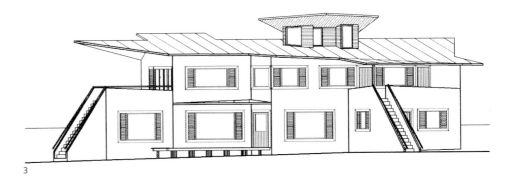

3

5

1 Continuous movement of light washes rough zigzag walls
2 Exterior, showing rambling nature of building
3 North elevation
4 View of Andes mountains between roof overhang and terrace wall
5 Interior of house provides opportunities for endless wandering

Photography: Guy St. Claire

CASTLE CREEK LODGE

Aspen, Colorado, USA

42|40 Architecture Inc, formerly Urban Design Group/Denver and Chicago

1

2

3

4

5

1 House as part of landscape

2 Loggia

3 Elevation

4 End elevation at night

5 Garage detail

Photography: Greg Hursley, Photographer

6 Entry porch

7 Upstairs gallery

8 Gallery and totem

9 Great room

10 Stair and gallery

Photography: Greg Hursley, Photographer

8

9

10

CH HOUSE

La Garriga, Barcelona, Spain

Jordi Badia, Mercè Sangenis (BAAS)

1

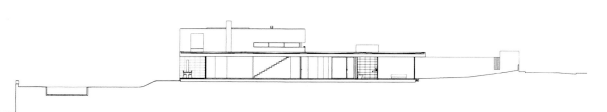

1 Lateral view of house with longitudinal opening and displaced wall of bath

2 Night view from outside kitchen

3 Elevation

4 View of house from swimming pool

5 Night view

Photography: Eugeni Pons

3

2

4

5

6

7

8

9

6　Perspective drawing of central courtyard

7　Volume of main bathroom, wood covered, with dressing room beyond

8　View of central courtyard with lavender and lemon tree

9　View of living room with stair access to study and courtyard beyond

Photography: Eugeni Pons

CONCRETE POLL HOUSE

Perth, Western Australia, Australia

Gary Marinko Architects

1

1 View from main courtyard of living room illuminated by kitchen light walls

2 Street façade of house at night from entrance courtyard

3 View of dining and living rooms, illuminated by kitchen light walls; bedroom courtyard is beyond

4 View of main courtyard from kitchen

5 View along entrance passage with light coming through front door and skylight over

Photography: The Cat's Pyjamas, Jacqueline Stevenson

2

3

4

5

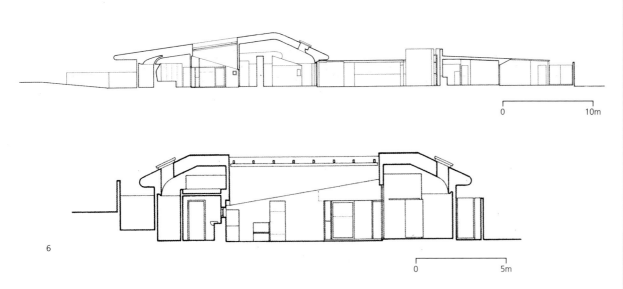

6

7

8

9

Photography: The Cat's Pyjamas, Jacqueline Stevenson

10

CONNECTICUT RESIDENCE

Connecticut, USA

Elliott + Associates Architects

2

3

4

6

5

4 Family room fireplace with Ernst blocks and sandblasted stainless
     steel television cabinet

5 Master bedroom looking toward master bath

6 Living room looking toward dining room

7 Master bath looking north

8 Floor plan

Photography: Bob Shimer/Hedrich-Blessing

7

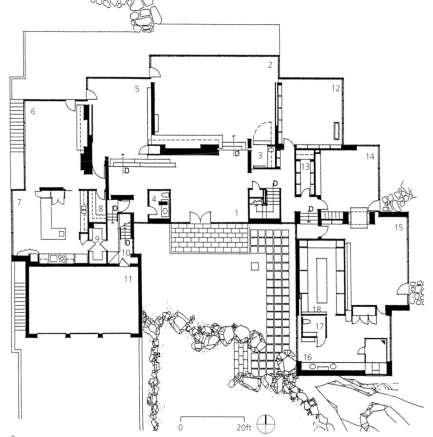

8

1	Entry	10	Stair
2	Living	11	Garage
3	Bar	12	Study
4	Powder	13	Storage
5	Dining	14	Study
6	Family	15	Master bedroom
7	Kitchen	16	Master bath
8	Pantry	17	Toilet
9	Pantry	18	Closet

0   20ft

COROMANDEL BACH

Coromandel, New Zealand

Crosson Clarke Architects

1

2

3

4

1 A stage for living

2 Open tent-like living space

3 Warm, natural interior at dusk

4 Open fireplace and plywood for winter occupation

Photography: Patrick Reynolds

5

7

6

8

9

5   Habitable 'box', overlooking the sea

6   Shower and bathroom open to the sun and the view, inviting the breeze

7   Deck folded down and solid natural walls reminiscent of early trip dams in the area

8   Textured container settled behind grassy hill

9   Timber shutters, natural timber weatherboards and exterior structure

Photography: Patrick Reynolds

CORUM RESIDENCE

Pella, Iowa, USA

Herbert Lewis Kruse Blunck Architecture

1

2

3

4

5

6

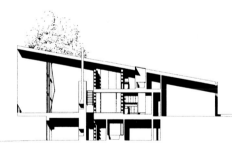

7

1   Twilight view

2   Elevation across pond

3   Front view

4   Side view

5   View from master bedroom

6   View of dining and living areas

7   Section

Photography: Shimer/Hedrich-Blessing

1

2

3

4

1 Main entry
2 Living room
3 Dining
4 Kitchen
5 Study
6 Bathroom 1
7 Bathroom 2
8 Master bedroom
9 Dressing room
10 Bedroom 2
11 Garage
12 Store
13 Cellar

5

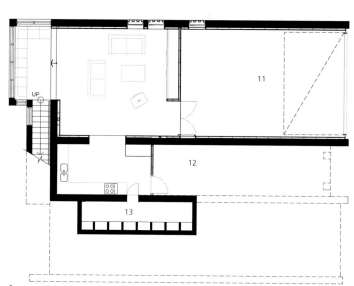

6

7

8

1 Front façade, main entry

2 Rear external façade

3 Internal open plan living/kitchen/dining area

4 Living area joinery is streamlined and free of unnecessary detail

5 Lower ground floor plan

6 Ground floor plan

7 New kitchen features bianco Carrara marble, walnut veneer and colorbacked glass

8 Internal open-plan living area

Photography: Adam Bruzzone

DALWHINNIE

Queenstown, New Zealand

Murray Cockburn Partnership

2

3

4

Opposite:
View to west from house parking area,
400 meters above Lake Wakatipu

2 Aerial view from north of front entrance
and Lake Wakatipu below

3 Aerial view from southeast shows house
nestled into cliffside

4 Mid-winter view of north aspect and
front entrance from driveway

Photography: Dale Gardiner (1,4); A. Brooks (2,3)

5　Entrance hallway with view of spiral stairs through drumtower window

6　Mid-level entrance to spiral stairs from front entrance hallway

7　Dining area and kitchen

8　Upper level floor plan

9　Mid level floor plan

10　Lower level floor plan

11　The Eyrie with semi-circular desk and 180-degree view of lake and mountains

12　The Nook is a cozy area for TV viewing

13　Views of the Remarkables Range and Lake Wakatipu from master bedroom

Photography: Dale Gardiner

5

6

7

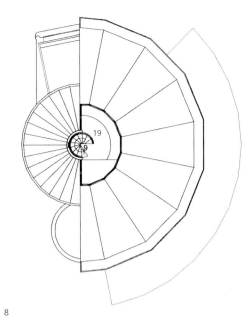

8

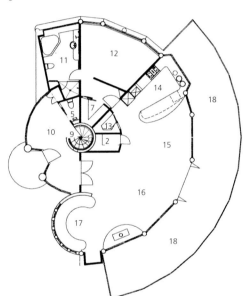

9

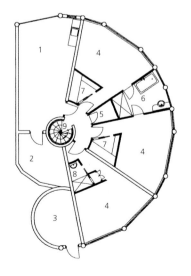

10

1 Garage
2 Store
3 Tank room
4 Bedroom
5 WC
6 Bathroom
7 Dressing
8 Shower
9 Stair
10 Entry
11 Ensuite bathroom
12 Master bedroom
13 Pantry
14 Kitchen
15 Dining
16 Living
17 Nook
18 Deck
19 Eyrie

11

12

13

DESERT RESIDENCE

Rancho Mirage, California, USA

Olson Sundberg Kundig Allen Architects

3

4

2

Opposite:

Interior opens to outside

2 Informal breakfast/dining room

3 View toward entry; interior spaces are arranged along a central gallery

4 Media room

5 Long and low, the house complements surrounding landscape

Photography: Dominique Vorillon (1–4); Cindy Anderson (5)

5

EDGEWATER

Short Hills, New Jersey, USA

WESKetch Architecture

2

3

Opposite:

Northwest side perspective

2 North elevation

3 Front entry with main stair tower

4 Southeast view

5 Side entry

Photography: Jay Rosenblatt Photography

4

5

Edgewater **75**

6 Foyer

7 Kitchen

8 Family room with custom trusses

Photography: Jay Rosenblatt Photography

8

EQUIS HOUSE

La Escondida Beach, Cañete, Peru

Barclay & Crousse Architecture

1

2

3

1 Entrance patio

2 Public space between Equis House and M House

3 Master bedroom loggia

4 Terrace and pool

5 Living/dining looking north

6 Living/dining looking south

7 Staircase from pool, looking east

8 Terrace and pool from dining/living entry

Photography: J.P. Crousse

FIRE ISLAND HOUSE

Fire Island Pines, New York, USA

Roger Hirsch, Architect, Susan Frostén, Architect, Drew Souza, Designer

2

Opposite:
   Glass façade fills double-height space with northern light

2   Orange wall creates privacy and defines entry path

3   A recovered 1951 'Juicy Fruit' billboard adds color to kitchen wall

4   Master bedroom with pivoting panel overlooks living room and pool

5   Linear skylight admits a slice of sun into living room

Photography: Michael Moran

4

3

5

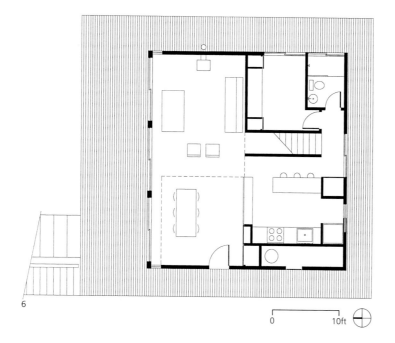

6   Ground floor plan, with living/dining area, kitchen, guest room and bath

7   Living room view with scrim panel partially concealing kitchen

8   Open stairs and translucent scrim allow views through house

9   Kitchen with brushed stainless counters and maple cabinets

Photography: Michael Moran

Opposite:

View from water side with bedroom wing to right

2   Entry with two benches is tucked under a wide eave

3   South deck joins water and garden sides of house

4   A covered porch wraps south side of house

5   Upper and lower bathrooms have an outdoor
    copper-wrapped shower and changing area

Photography: Michael Mathers

2

3

4

5

6

6 A ship's ladder to a reading loft is built into dining side of fireplace

7 Kitchen and dining room flow out into deck

8 A small reading loft is located over the kitchen

9 End of living room frames a small, open stair

10 First floor plan

Photography: Michael Mathers

7

8

9

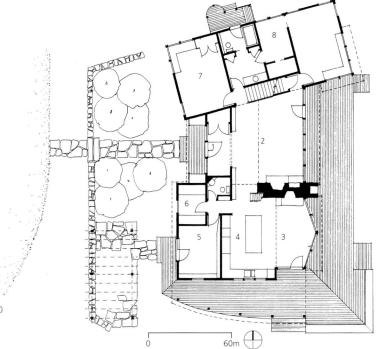

10

1 Entry
2 Living
3 Dining
4 Kitchen
5 Study
6 Laundry
7 Bedroom
8 Bedroom

0   60m

GAMA ISSA HOUSE

Alto de Pinheiros, São Paulo, Brazil

Marcio Kogan Architect

2

Opposite:

Double-height living room opens to outdoors

2 Main façade

Photography: Arnaldo Pappalardo

3

4

3 Dining room

4 Shower detail

5 Main façade at night

Opposite:
  Rear façade and studio

Photography: Arnaldo Pappalardo

5

GILLESPIE RESIDENCE

Vancouver, British Columbia, Canada

James K.M. Cheng Architects Inc.

2

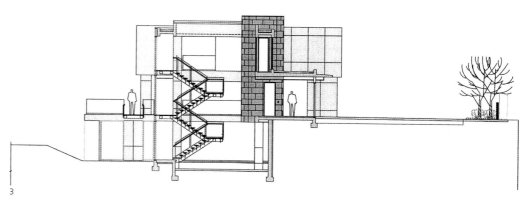

3

4

5 Atrium with glass and steel stair

6 Dining/living room

7 Living room and entry

8 Atrium toward dining/living room

Photography: Martin Tessler

GLAZER RESIDENCE

Colorado, USA

Appleton & Associates, Inc. – Architects

1 Main compound; silo entry stair tower is
   center left

2 House from across meadow, showing
   mountain view setting

3 Exterior showing major materials

4 Exterior, with spa designed as a well

Photography: Alex Vertikoff

2

3

4

5

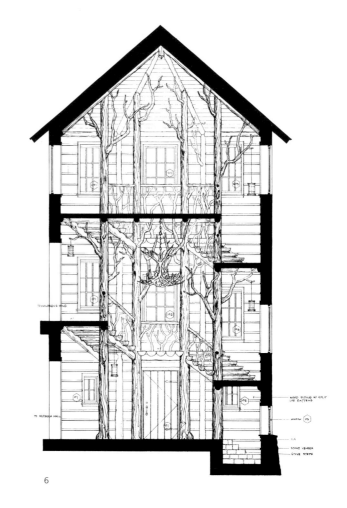

6

7

8

9

10

GLENCOE RESIDENCE

Venice, California, USA

Marmol Radziner and Associates

3

Opposite:
View from rear of property, looking toward pool

2 Master bedroom

3 Swimming pool

4 Exterior view

5 Kitchen, looking toward outside fireplace

Photography: Benny Chan

2

4

5

Glencoe Residence **101**

Opposite:
Living room, with furniture designed by architect

6   First floor plan

7   Second floor plan

Photography: Benny Chan

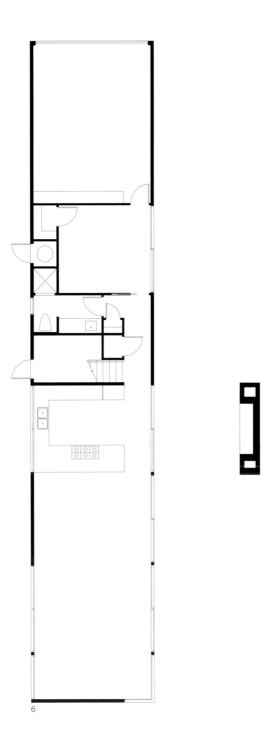

6

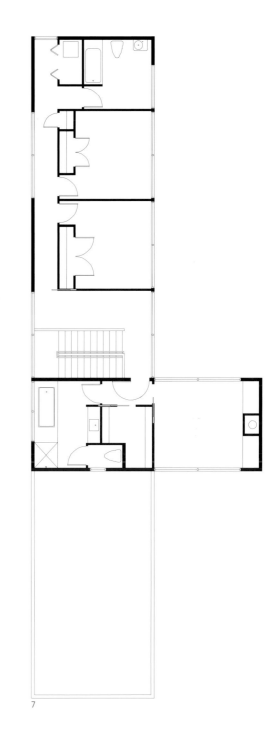

7

GOSLINE RESIDENCE

Washington, USA

Bohlin Cywinski Jackson

1 View from northeast
2 Main stair treads thread into maple wall slats
3 Polycarbonate screen stretches from exterior to interior
4 East elevation at dusk

Photography: Ben Benschnider (1,3,4); Karl Backus (2)

2

3

4

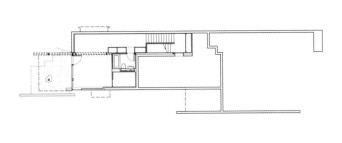

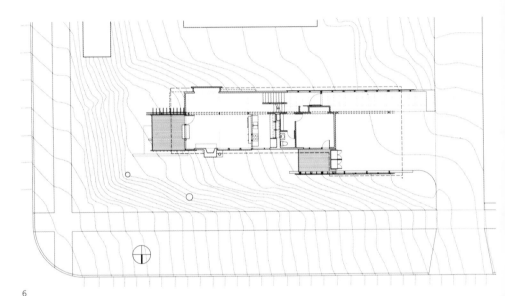

6

5

7

8

9

5   Main entry approach

6   Floor plans

7   Living room fireplace featuring steel-plate cladding

8   Two-story living room corner window frames view of Deodar cedar

9   Main living space with sleeping loft above

10 View from bedroom loft

Photography: Ben Benschnider (5,9); Karl Backus (7,8,10)

10

HINGE HOUSE

Los Angeles, California, USA

Aleks Istanbullu Architects

2

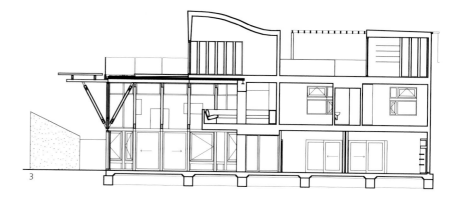

3

4

Opposite:
Colorful and fun, the house is fit for an animator

2 Terrace off master suite leads to spa

3 Section

4 'Hinged' space encourages outdoor and indoor living

Photography: Weldon Brewster

5

7

6

5 Open living space includes indoor koi pond
and inventive lighting

6 Screening room is de rigueur for
entertainment executives

7 Spacious kitchen with translucent backsplash

8 Entry to master suite is playful; fish tank is
bedroom wall

9 Dining area is part of first-floor open space

Photography: Weldon Brewster

8

9

HOUSE ON THE HILL

Serra da Mantiqueira, Brazil

Carlos Bratke

2

3

4

Opposite:
  Front view
2   Lateral elevation study
3   Rear view
4   Lateral view
Photography: José Moscardi Jr

5

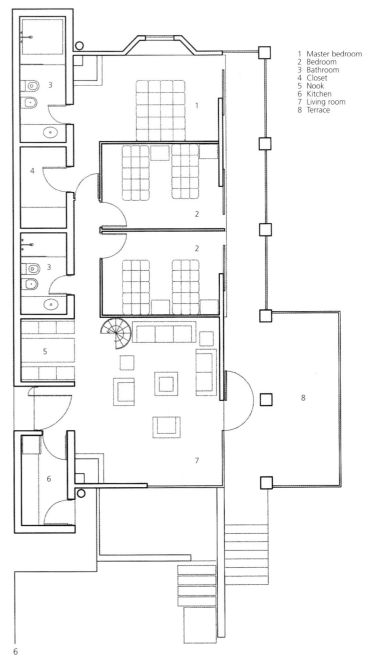

6

1 Master bedroom
2 Bedroom
3 Bathroom
4 Closet
5 Nook
6 Kitchen
7 Living room
8 Terrace

7

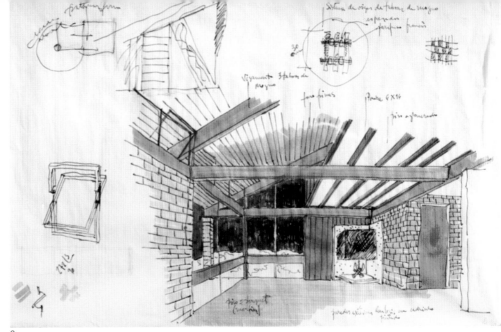

8

9

5   View of terrace
6   Floor plan
7&9   Living room interior
8   Living room study

Photography: José Moscardi Jr

HOUSE OTTO

Bergheim, Salzburg, Austria

Peter Ebner + Franziska Ullmann

1

2

3

4

5

1 View from living room to dining room

2 View from master bedroom to master bathroom

3 Sun terrace

4 South elevation, breakfast terrace

5 View outside master bedroom

6 View from children's bedroom to mountains beyond

7 Dining room

8 Underground area inside courtyard

9 Home office with view of Gaisberg mountain

Photography: Margherita Spillutini

HOUSE R 128

Stuttgart, Germany

Werner Sobek

1

2

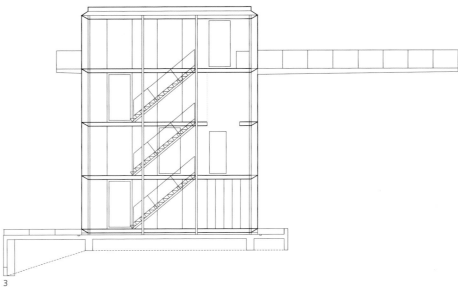

3

4

5

Opposite:
East elevation at dusk

2 North elevation

3 Section

4 Vertical access

5 Living/dining area

Photography: Roland Halbe

ISLAND HOUSE

St. Lawrence River, Ontario, Canada

Shim-Sutcliffe Architects

Opposite:
   View of north elevation with clover meadow in foreground

2 Site plan

3 Night view of reflecting pool with house beyond

4 View of cubic living room

5 View of reflecting pool with living room beyond

Photography: James Dow

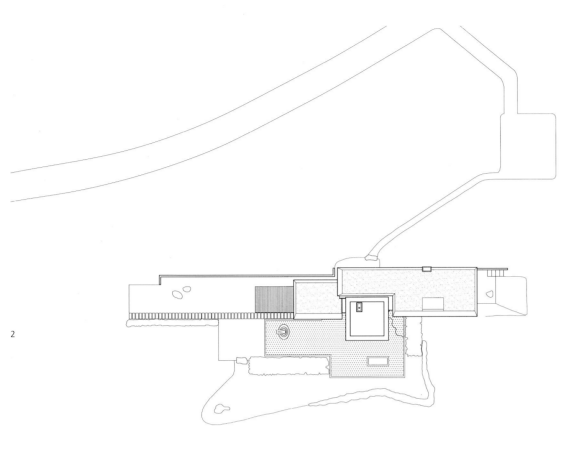

2

4

3

5

6   Ground floor plan
7   View of entrance with cubic volume of living room to left
8   Living room seen from dining area
9   View of entrance area with upper portion of living room to right
10 View of reflecting pool, living room, and St. Lawrence River
    beyond from private outdoor deck

Photography: James Dow

8

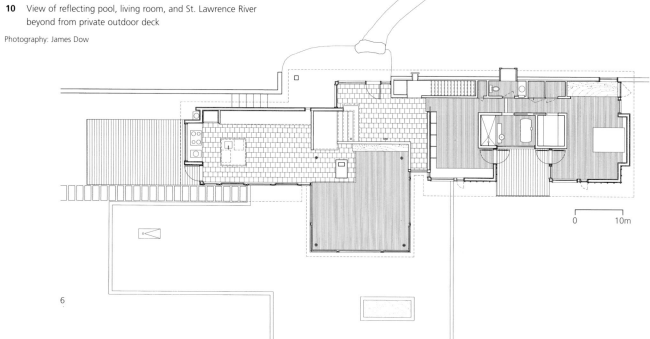

6

0   10m

7

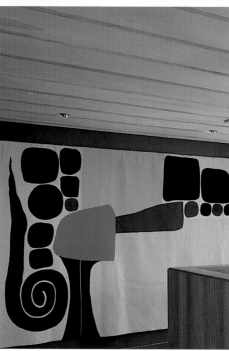

9

10

JONES RESIDENCE

Manhattan Beach, California, USA

SFJones Architects Inc.

1

1 West view from street

2 View of main space showing axial connection to other spaces

3 View of kitchen

4 View showing spatial relationship between kitchen, family room and exterior

Photography: Weldon Brewster

Jones Residence 125

KANGALOON HOUSE

New South Wales, Australia

Peter Stronach, Allen Jack + Cottier

1

1 Twilight view of north elevation reveals unique character of main living spaces

2 Vernacular rural architectural form and materials; barn, verandah, shed, and corrugated iron used to great effect

3 Solidity/cloistered spaces of top floor relative to openness and transparency of ground floor

Photography: Peter Hyatt

2

3

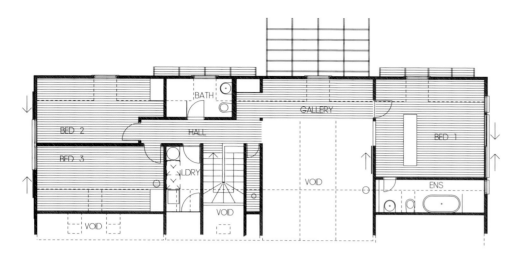

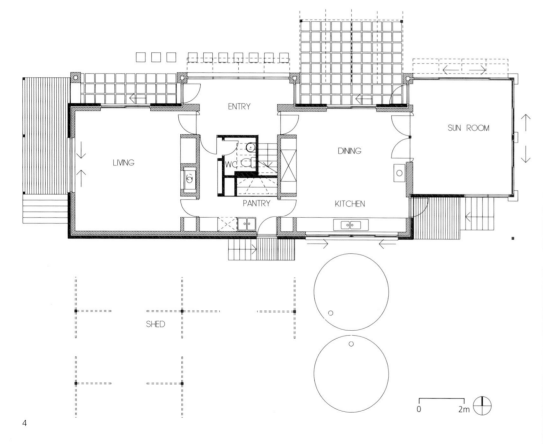

BED 2

BED 3

VOID

BATH

HALL

LDRY

VOID

GALLERY

VOID

BED 1

ENS

LIVING

ENTRY

WC

PANTRY

DINING

KITCHEN

SUN ROOM

SHED

0   2m

4

5

4 Floor plans: first floor, ground floor

5 Two-story, open-plan kitchen/dining room provides feeling of spaciousness with double-height ceilings and open space vistas

6 Traditional farmhouse dormers and ceilings add interest to bedroom

7 Sunroom; large glass doors between spaces allow areas to be closed off for winter efficiency

Photography: Peter Hyatt

6

7

KILBURN RESIDENCE

Western Australia, Australia

Iredale Pedersen Hook Architects

2

3

4

5

KIMBER HOUSE

Perth, Western Australia, Australia

Patroni Architects

1

2

4

3

1 Timber deck over water garden to main street entrance

2 North view over pool to tennis court beyond

3 North elevation from tennis court

4 'Tramline wall' element with pool

Photography: Robert Frith

5

7

6

5   Family living areas open onto pool deck

6   Stair and balustrade furniture elements

7   Polished concrete stair plinth

8   Kitchen in family living area

9   Entry from street

10   Main bedroom and dressing room

11   Dressing area adjacent to main bedroom

Photography: Robert Frith

8

9

10

11

LEESA AND SAM'S HOUSE

Christmas Lake, Excelsior, Minnesota, USA

Charles R. Stinson Architects

1

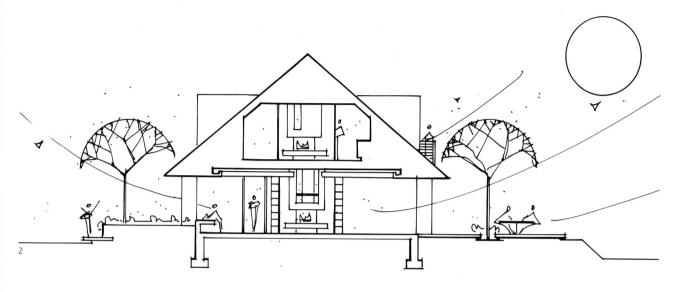

Photography: Peter Bastinelli Kerze

2

3

4

5

6

7

4 Stairs

5 Dining room

6 Master bedroom

7 Hallway

8 View to lounge room

9 Relax room

Photography: Peter Bastinelli Kerze

8

9

LEXTON MACCARTHY RESIDENCE

Silver Lake, California, USA

Lorcan O'Herlihy Architects

1

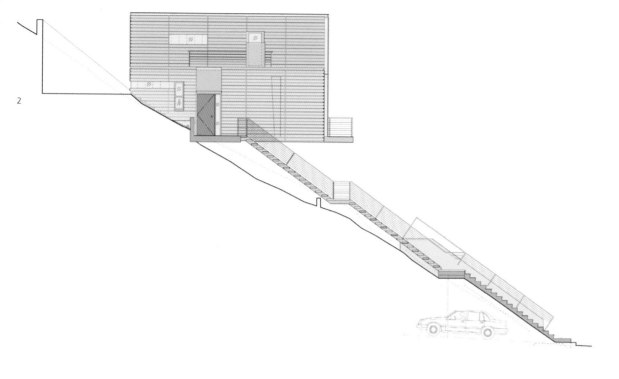

1 View from street at dusk

2 North elevation

3 Rear elevation

4 Corner window detail

5 View from roof deck of Los Feliz and Hollywood

Photography: Douglas Hill

4

3

5

Lexton MacCarthy Residence **141**

6

7

8

9

11

10

6   View of glass façade

7   Living room

8   Work space

9   Exterior view of building; 1x6 wood siding

10 Master bedroom

11 Living room; 1x6 wood siding through fixed glazing

Photography: Douglas Hill

LOVALL VALLEY RESIDENCE

Napa County, California, USA

Cass Calder Smith Architecture

1

2

3

4

5

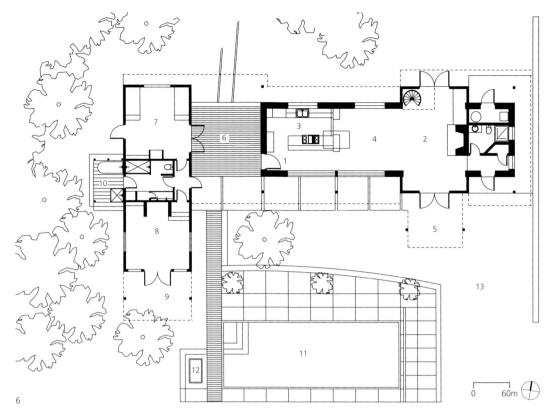

6

7

1 Entry
2 Living
3 Kitchen
4 Dining
5 East arbor
6 Breezeway
7 Kids' bedroom
8 Master bedroom
9 West arbor
10 Outdoor bath
11 Pool
12 Jacuzzi
13 Garden

0   60m

1   Breezeway view from lawn and pool

2   Fireplace and living room from dining area

3   Sleeping loft with view to south

4   House set amongst contours and forest

5   South side of house with pool and landscaping

6   Ground floor plan

7   Kitchen counter, shelves and window

8   Kitchen and dining area from living room

Photography: David Duncan Livingston

8

M HOUSE

La Escondida Beach, Cañete, Peru

Barclay & Crousse Architecture

1

2

3

1 Inside and outside spaces merge into one in living area
2 Entry alley and living space from pool
3 Loggia from entry alley frames ocean view
4 Working sketch of living space
5 View of house from Pacific Ocean
6 Integration of abstract volumes
7 Exterior view of entry from access route

Photography: Roberto Huarcaya, Jean Pierre Crousse

MAISON KATZ–RENIERS

Rue des Pêcheurs, Brussels, Belgium

Victor Lévy, Architect

1

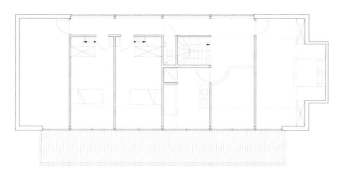

2

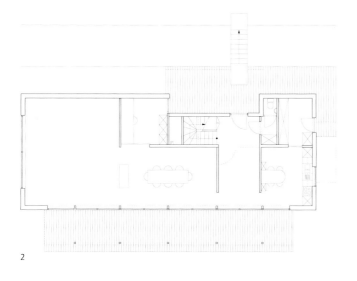

1 Entrance
2 Floor plans: ground floor, first floor
3 Hallway on first floor
4 Master bedroom

Photography: Marie-Françoise Plissart

3

4

Photography: Marie-Françoise Plissart

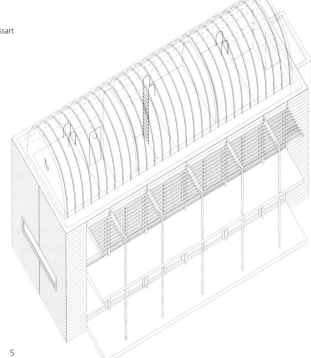

5

6

7

8

150

9

10

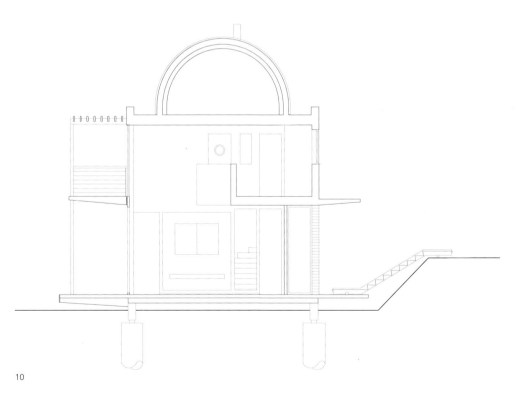

MALIBU RESIDENCE

Malibu, California, USA

Shubin + Donaldson Architects

1

4

1 Rear of house opens onto famed Malibu beach from living room below and master suite above

2 Transitional interior courtyard

3 Dining room is framed with white-gridded windows

4 Kitchen is open to first-floor living and dining areas

Photography: Tom Bonner

6

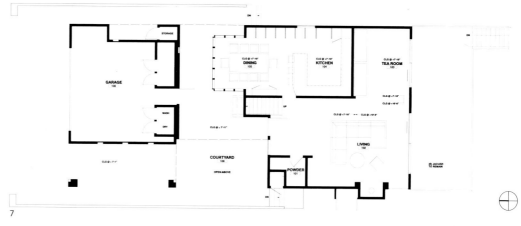

7

5   White, comfortable furniture adds to informality of a beach house

6   Master bath is spa-like with frosted glass and wenge wood

7   First floor plan

8   Sleeping porch is ultimate expression of outdoor living

Photography: Tom Bonner

8

MANKINS-CAMP RESIDENCE

San Francisco, California, USA

Herbert Lewis Kruse Blunck Architecture

1

2

3

4

5

6

7

8

1 Lower level sitting area with view beyond
2 Master bedroom with dressing and master bath beyond
3 Living area from dining area
4 Living area with dining area beyond
5 Living area/fireplace
6 Stair with view beyond
7 Entry view
8 Master bath

Photography: Farshid Assassi/Assassi Productions

MASON HOUSE

Sydney, New South Wales, Australia

Chenchow Little Architects

2

1

3

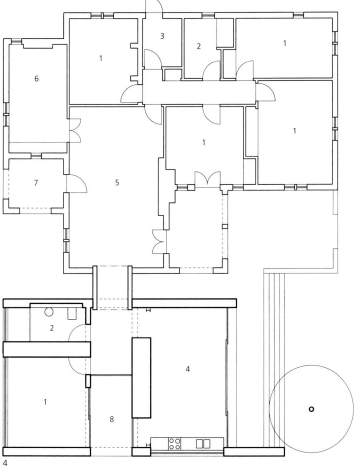

1 Bedroom
2 Bathroom
3 Laundry
4 Kitchen/dining
5 Living
6 Study
7 Entry
8 Court

4

1 East elevation

2 North elevation

3 Detail of north elevation

4 Floor plan

5&6 Eat-in kitchen

7 Master bedroom and central terrace viewed from hallway

Photography: Anthony Browell – Okidoki

5

6

7

MATCHBOX HOUSE

North Fork, Long Island, New York, USA

Gluckman Mayner Architects

1

2

3

4

1 Interior view of stair
2 Exterior front façade at dusk
3 Exterior view, rear of house
4 View of deck
5 Exterior view, front façade
6 Longitudinal section
7 Living room
8 Entrance to living room

Photography: Melinda Buie/Gluckman Mayner Architects

5

6

7

8

MONTECITO RESIDENCE

Montecito, California, USA

Shubin + Donaldson Architects

2

3

4

Opposite:

One of few contemporary homes in
a traditional area

2   Industrial materials form poetic entrance

3   Louvered structure protects from the sun

4   Exterior elements punctuate interior

Photography: Tom Bonner

Montecito Residence   **163**

5

6

8

7

5   Cherry and marble kitchen is open to seating area and views

6   Shed roof continues from outside to inside

7   Corridors double as art galleries

8   Expansive living space is divided by custom fireplace

Photography: Tom Bonner

MONTECITO HILLSIDE RESIDENCE

Montecito, California, USA

Ronald Frink Architects

Oppposite:
   Exterior with infinity-edged pool and terrace, facing north

2 Living room with Santa Barbara Harbor and ocean view

3 Kitchen with view to family entertainment area

4 Entry court at twilight

Photography: Erhard Pfeiffer

2

3

4

5

6

7

8

5   Main house, master study from stair hall
6   Her master bath, second floor with tree-top views
7   Living room with view to dining and gallery
8   Guest house interior, first-floor seating area
9   Bridge to guest house

Photography: Erhard Pfeiffer (5–8); Benny Chan, fotoworks (9)

9

Montecito Hillside Residence   **169**

MOUNTAIN TREE HOUSE

Dillard, Georgia, USA

Mack Scogin Merrill Elam Architects

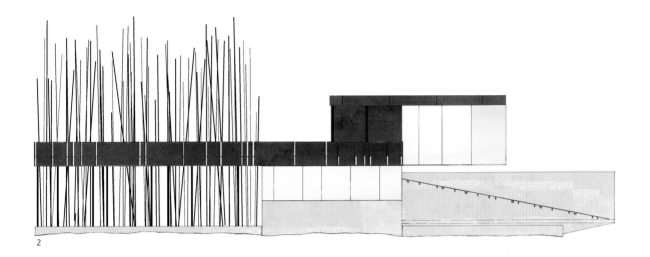

2

3

5

4

Opposite:
Mountain Tree House

2 South elevation

3 Arrival view across pond

4 View to south from junction of ramp and bamboo deck

5 View from northeast

Photography: Timothy Hursley, The Arkansas Office

Photography: Timothy Hursley, The Arkansas Office

6

7

8

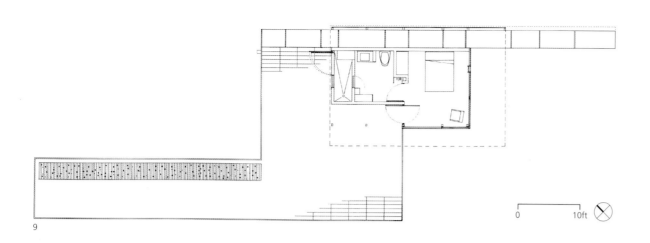

9

10

11

12

NEW HOUSE

Paraparaumu, Kapiti Coast, New Zealand

Bevin + Slessor Architects

1

2

3

4

6

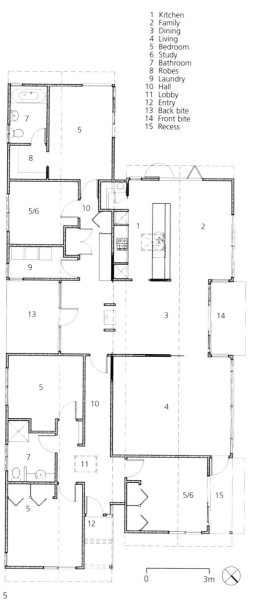

1 Kitchen
2 Family
3 Dining
4 Living
5 Bedroom
6 Study
7 Bathroom
8 Robes
9 Laundry
10 Hall
11 Lobby
12 Entry
13 Back bite
14 Front bite
15 Recess

0   3m

5

1 West facing, the house nestles between paddock and bush

2 Approaching front door from north

3 Central dining area opens out to front 'bite'

4 Plywood, cedar, aluminum, concrete, gravel and steel

5 Floor plan

6 Looking from back bite and fireplace to west

7 Timber-floored dining area flows through to family area

8 Timber is used to both shade and ventilate

Photography: Ric Slessor

7

8

ORTEGA RIDGE RESIDENCE

Summerland, California, USA

B3 Architects, a Berkus Design Studio

1

2

3

1 Courtyard elevation: block sentinels capped with glass clerestories illuminate passageways
2 View of main art gallery from central tower
3 Sunken lounge with glass, wood and limestone texture
4 Sculpted limestone and copper forms floating in courtyard

Photography: Peter Malinowski

4

PALM DESERT RESIDENCE

California, USA

B3 Architects, a Berkus Design Studio

2

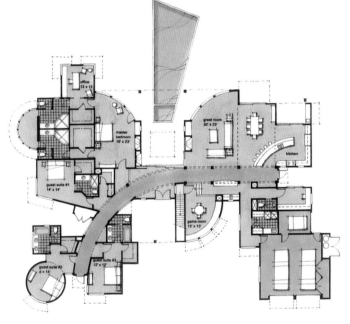

4

Opposite:
Centrally located pool divides formal and informal living zones

2 Entry elevation: sculpted geometric forms pay homage to desert surroundings

3 Curving interior hallway functions as a main street and gallery

4 Floor plan

Photography: Farshid Assassi

3

Palm Desert Residence **179**

PALO ALTO HOUSE

Palo Alto, California, USA

Swatt Architects

Opposite:
   View through gallery to rear yard
2 Floating stair with suspended glass and stainless steel railing system
3 Lower level floor plan
4 Night view of 'public' kitchen/dining areas
Photography: Cesar Rubio

5

6

7

5   Dining room with library and glass bridge above

6   Upper level of gallery

7   Circulation space at kitchen/breakfast areas

8   Gallery curtain wall at night

9   Master bedroom

10 View of front entry courtyard

Photography: Cesar Rubio

9

8

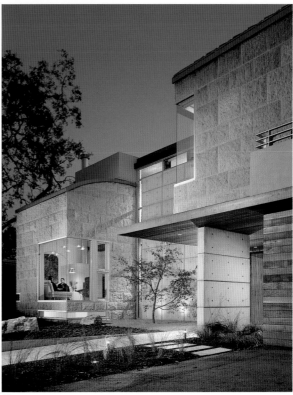

10

PARK PRESIDIO RESIDENCE

San Francisco, California, USA

Kuth Ranieri Architects

1

2

3

4

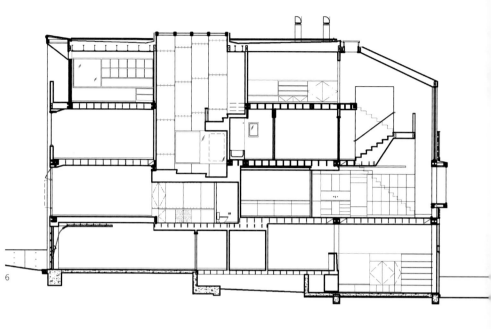

6

8

1 Bridge at master suite

2 Back façade

3 Front façade

4 Stairwell

5 Main level hallway

6 Section

7 Master bathroom

8 Dining area

Photography: courtesy Kuth Ranieri Architects

7

PRIVATE RESIDENCE

Wyoming, USA

Dubbe-Moulder Architects

2

3

Opposite:
Kitchen, with views of mountain scenery

5 Guest cabin's natural setting and double-sided fireplace

6 Guest cabin living room is cozy and comfortable

Photography: The Seen, Cameron R. Neilson

5

6

RANCHO DOS VIDAS

Frio County, Texas, USA

Michael G. Imber, Architect

3

4

1 Hunting lodge kitchen
2 Hunting lodge living room
3 Second bedroom
4 Master suite
5 Interior plaster groin vault at entry court

Photography: Jack Thompson (1,2,4,5); Paul Bardagjy (3)

5

6

7

8

9

10

11

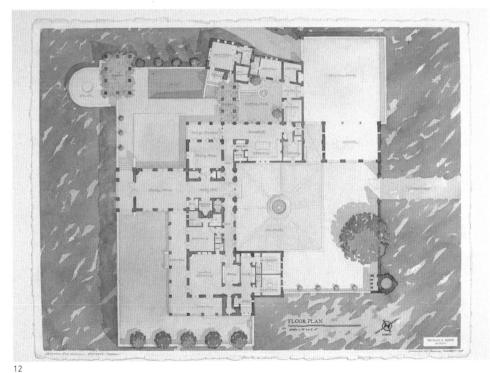

12

6 Porte cochere off entry court

7 Approach to ranch through south Texas sendero

8 Pool loggia

9 Entry court at sunset

10 Entry court from bedroom window

11 Pergola

12 Site plan

Photography: Jack Thompson (6–9,11); Paul Bardagjy (10)

RANGER POINT HOUSE

Seatoun, Wellington, New Zealand

New Work Studio

Opposite:

Looking through sliding doors into ground floor living and dining area, fireplace, and stair beyond

2 View from across rocky foreshore of Breaker Bay to the house in context, with old beachside cottages and bungalows, and steep hill behind

3 Exterior view at night, showing transparency of house through windows and plastic sheeting

4 Street frontage and east elevation, showing entry, with recycled weatherboards on garage

Photography: Paul McCredie, courtesy *NZ Home & Entertainment* (1–3); Mark Hadfield (4)

5

6

7

8

5 Top floor main bedroom with handrail to void over stair in foreground

6 Kitchen space, with floating stainless steel bench, and raw steel wall lining behind wet area

7 Looking across dining table toward kitchen

8 Entry view, double-height with stair in recycled jarrah, plywood, grooved custom wood lining

Photography: Paul McCredie, courtesy *NZ House and Garden* (5,6); Mark Hadfield (7,8)

RESIDENCE AND ATELIER

Umyeon-dong, Seoul, South Korea

Kim Young-Sub + Kunchook-Moonhwa Architect Associates

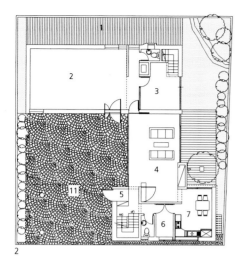

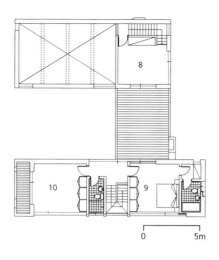

2

1 Outdoor workshop	7 Kitchen/dining room
2 Atelier	8 Guest room
3 Library	9 Master bedroom
4 Living room	10 Children's room
5 Entrance	11 Parking
6 Laundry	

0   5m

4

3

Opposite:

Front view

2 Floor plan

3 Atelier gate

4 Gate and inner court (madang)

Photography: Lee Keehwan (1,4); Kim Jaekyeong (3)

Residence and Atelier **199**

5

5 Architect's sketch

6 View from neighbor (west side)

7 Upper-level wooden deck

Opposite:
View from madang

Photography: Lee Keehwan (6,7); Kim Young-Sub (Opposite)

6

7

RESIDENCE AT SANUR ELOK

Jakarta, Indonesia

Paramita Abirama Istasadhya, PT. (PAI)

1

2

3

1 Corner façade view

2 Family room connects to inner courtyard
with swimming pool

3 Main entry façade

4 Formal living room with view to formal
dining room

5 Sitting room with game table in foreground

6 Master bedroom suite

7 Study

Photography: Ir. Yori Antar (1–3); Iskandar Irawan (4–7)

4

5

6

7

RESIDENCE FOR A SCULPTOR 3

Santa Rosa, California, USA

Sander Architects

Opposite:
  East façade shows house lifted above hillside
  on steel frame pilotis

2   Prefabricated steel frame exposed on uphill
    (west) side

3   South view, house is perched above steeply
    sloped site

4   Entry is behind house along uphill side

Photography: Sharon Risedorph

5 Top half of torqued steel wall at entry vessel, as seen from Great Room

6 Great Room, with view toward Valley of the Moon. Display wall includes ceramic work by the owner and others.

7 ½-inch rusted steel wall, curved and torqued to enclose entry vessel

8 Entry vessel is conceived as a vertical, inward-focused gallery space

Photography: Sharon Risedorph

7

8

RESIDENCE ON VALENTINE CREEK

Crownsville, Maryland, USA

Good Architecture

2

3

4

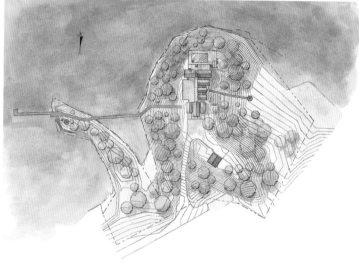

5

Opposite:

View of east elevation

2 View of chess tower from path along west side

3 View of covered entry and garages

4 Entry walk looking back at garage

5 Site plan

Photography: Celia Pearson

6

8

9

10

6 View of pool side elevation from inside chess tower

7 Master balcony

8 Kitchen

9 Entry foyer looking into river room beyond

10 Entry at twilight with main stair in view

Photography: Celia Pearson

Residence on Valentine Creek **211**

REYNOLDS RESIDENCE

Western Australia, Australia

Iredale Pedersen Hook Architects

1

2

3

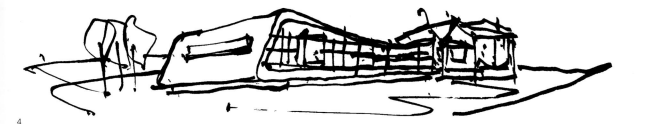

4

5

6

7

RUSKIN PLACE TOWNHOUSE

Seaside, Florida, USA

Alexander Gorlin Architects

2

3

Opposite:
    Profile of living room segment

2 Exterior support columns blend into interior
    glass-and-steel framework

3 Kitchen, located at rear of first floor

Photography: Peter Aaron/Esto

4

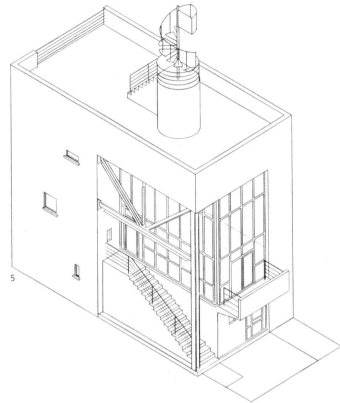

5

6

8

7

4 Glass-girded living room is dominated by Andreas
Feininger's 'Route 66' photograph

5 Axonometric

6 Master bedroom with internally lit headboard
covered in translucent plastic

7 Twilight view

8 Crow's nest on roof provides stunning views of
the Gulf of Mexico

Photography: Peter Aaron/Esto

RUSTIC CANYON RESIDENCE

Santa Monica, California, USA

A C Martin Partners

3

Opposite:

A play of geometric volumes belies an open, easy floor plan inside

2 Frosted-glass door introduces range of materials

3 Concrete is major building material

4 House complements the wooded site

Photography: John E. Linden

2

4

5

6

7

8

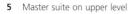
9

10

11

5   Master suite on upper level

6   Furniture includes modern masters

7   Light-filled volume shows art and furniture designed by architect

8   Master bath replete with Carrara marble

9   Open kitchen accented by art

10   Glass, steel, and wood are main materials

11   Elevator is masked behind frosted glass

Photography: John E. Linden

SANTA ANA HOUSE

Santa Ana, Costa Rica

Arquitectura y Diseño SCGMT

1

1 Residence is planned around central patio area

2 Visual elements, created with furniture and lighting, appear at the end of all corridors

3 Social areas of residence are very open and feature different ceiling designs

4 Main façade features arches, a common element throughout the house

Photography: Revista Estilos y Casas

2

3

4

SCREENED HOUSE

Fire Island Pines, New York, USA

Bromley Caldari Architects

1

1 View of entry court
2 Kitchen
3 Main space with screened porch
4 Screened porch
5 Bedroom
6 Floor plan

Photography: Christian Richins

2

3

4

5

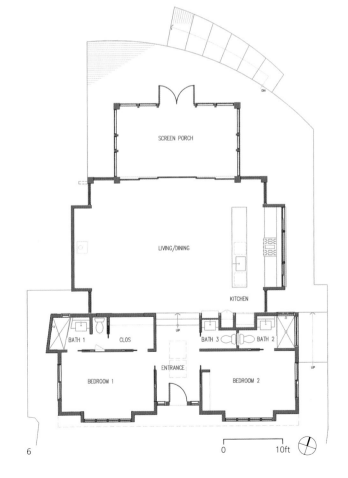

6

SERRANA HOUSE

Minas Gerais, Brazil

João Diniz Arquitetura Ltda

1

2

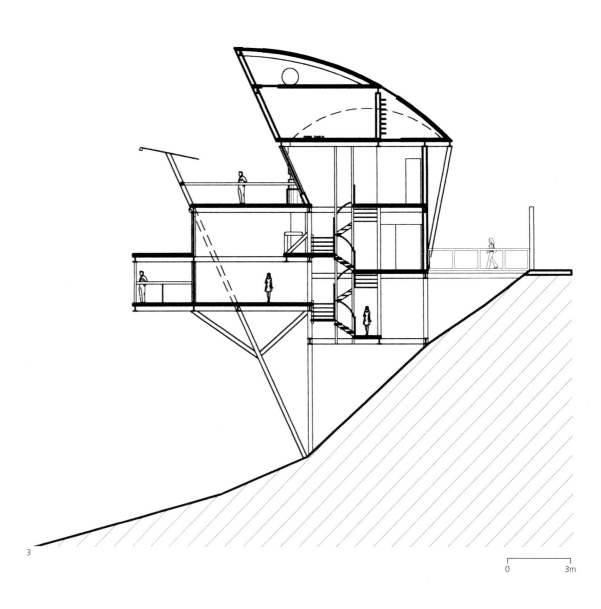

3

0   3m

4

5

1&2   House is designed to fit into surrounding topography

3   Section

4   Panoramic bathtub

5   Access bridge and structural architrave

6   Living room

7   Stair

Photography: Marcílio Gazzinelli

6

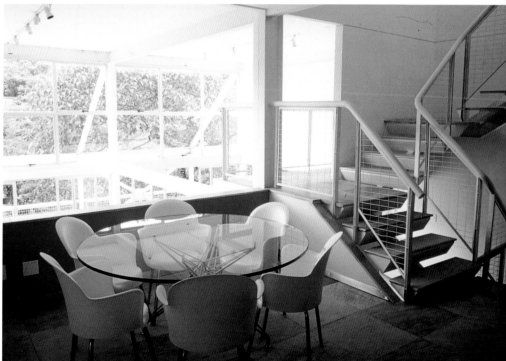
7

SEWELL RESIDENCE

Cedar Lake, Minnesota, USA

Charles R. Stinson Architects

1

2

3

1 Exterior view from street
2 View across Cedar Lake
3 Foyer/entry
4 Exterior view of entry
5 Great room

Photography: Peter Bastinelli Kerze

SIMMONDS-YIN RESIDENCE

Western Australia, Australia

Joe Chindarsi Architect

1

2

3

1 View from rear courtyard toward house shows seamless flow from inside to out and continuity of terrazzo tiles

2 Front entry slot has 11-foot-high (3.5-meter) translucent glass door leading to cherry-wood stair 'box' beyond

3 Front façade with silver birch forest presents a mask to street

Photography: Robert Frith, Acorn Photo Agency

4

5

7

6

4 View up stairs with mezzanine/study over; translucent window from ensuite hangs over space

5 Looking across half-unfolded dining bench to main living space with cherry-wood stair 'box' sliding past wall plane

6 Downstairs black bathroom—where the light is not

7 Looking out across daybed to rear courtyard and plunge pool with central liquid ambar tree

Photography: Robert Frith, Acorn Photo Agency

SIMPLICITY

Mustique, St. Vincent and the Grenadines

Diamond and Schmitt Architects Incorporated

2

Opposite:

   Courtyard through living room pavilion

2   Dining room

3&4   Living room pavilion verandah

Photography: Steven Evans

3

4

5

Photography: Steven Evans

6

7

8

9

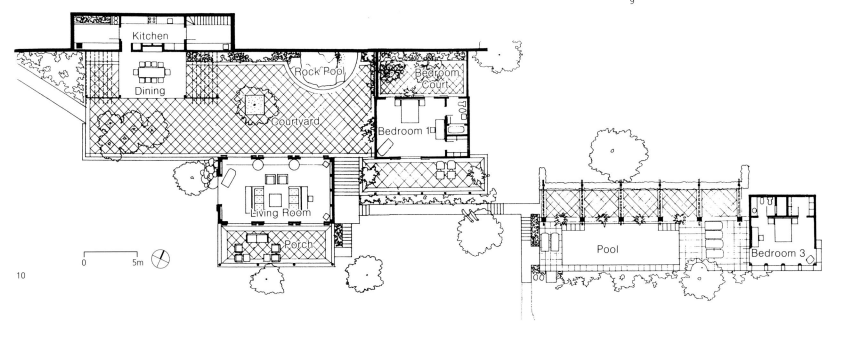

10

Kitchen

Dining

Rock Pool

Courtyard

Bedroom
Court

Bedroom 1

Living Room

Porch

Pool

Bedroom 3

0   5m

STABILIZED EARTH POLL HOUSE

Margaret River, Western Australia, Australia

Gary Marinko Architects

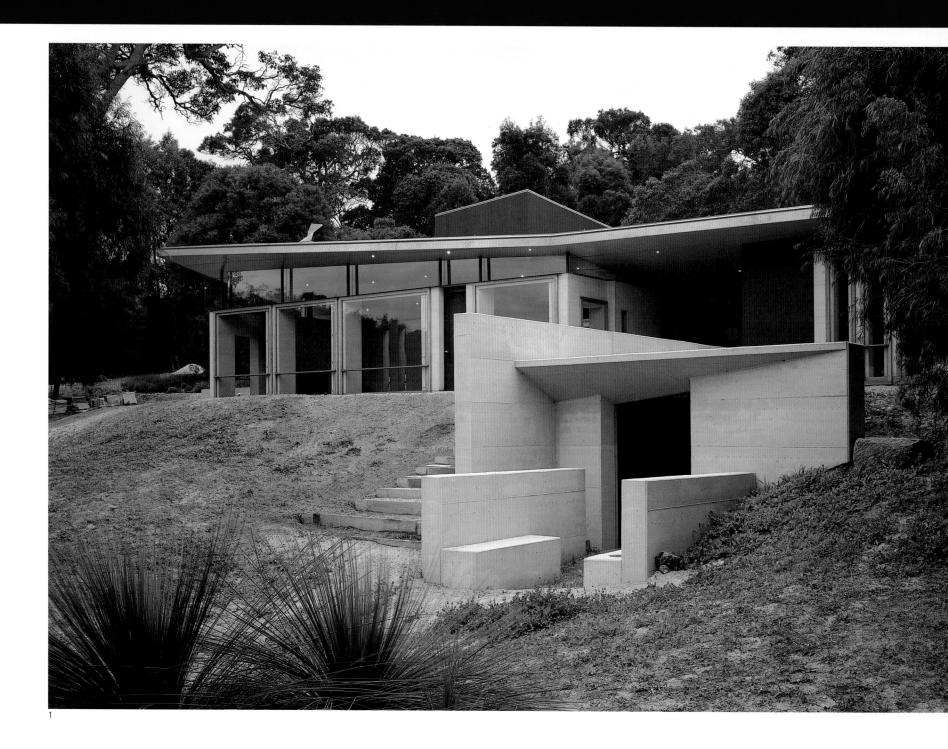

1

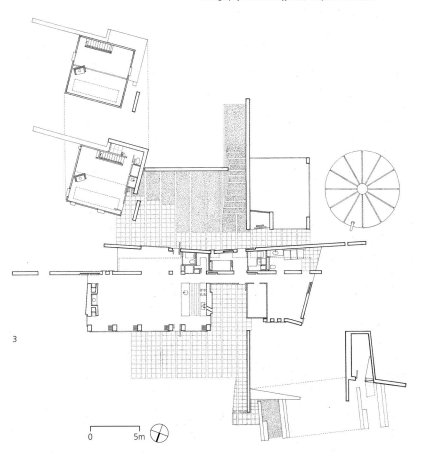

3

0   5m

2

5

4

Stabilized Earth Poll House **239**

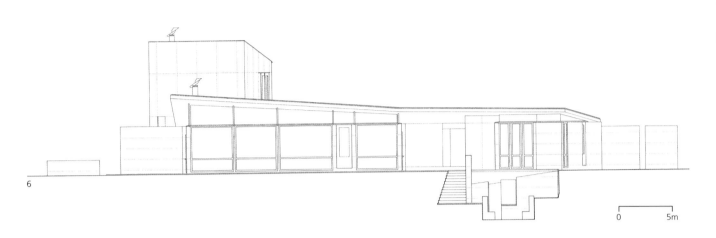

6

0   5m

8

7

9

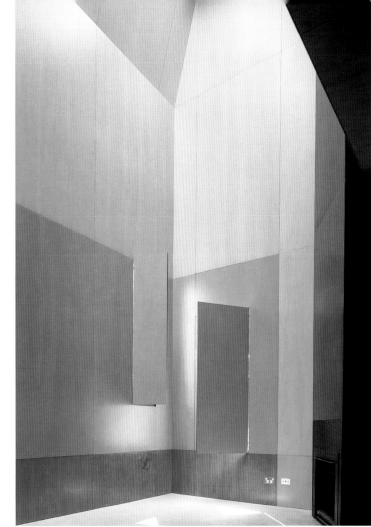

11

10

12

6   North elevation

7   View from hallway to living and dining room

8   View into study with cabinet door panels open

9   View of open shutters from living room

10   View into study with cabinet door panels closed

11   Studio interior from ground floor

12   Ensuite

Photography: The Cat's Pyjamas, Jacqueline Stevenson

STEINHARDT RESIDENCE

Birmingham, Michigan, USA

McIntosh Poris Associates

Opposite:
 Contemporary geometry makes a statement in
 this town of mostly traditional homes

2 Free-flow spaces from dining to living

3 Large windows give views from upper bedroom

4 Lower-level gym

Photography: Balthazar Korab

5

6

7

5 Sleek, contemporary furniture meshes with architecture

6 Terraces let owners enjoy indoor-outdoor living

7 Well-equipped kitchen flows easily to dining and living rooms

8 Loft-like space is reminiscent of New York living

Photography: Balthazar Korab

STUDIO HOUSE

Seattle, Washington, USA

Olson Sundberg Kundig Allen Architects

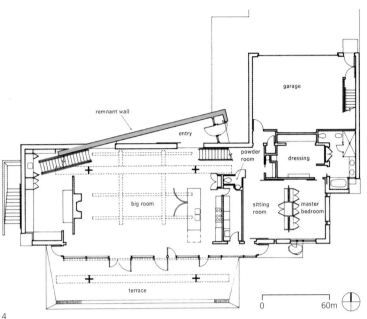

Opposite:

West façade; oversized steel beams, columns and door complement 'big room'

2 Entry gate and lantern; gate opens through entry canopy

3 General view of southwest corner

4 Main floor plan

5 Master bath; cantilevered concrete counter extends through window wall

Photography: Paul Warchol

5

6

7

5 Big terrace door opens to dining room

6 Photo wall with art image projection

7 Powder room; cabinet-like, the walls are varnished copper and plaster

8 View of 'big room' highlighting window wall

Photography: Paul Warchol

SUNRISE ROAD HOUSE

Palm Beach, New South Wales, Australia

Dawson Brown Architecture

1

3

2

4

5

6

7

1 North elevation of new house

2 North elevation of original house and pavilion addition

3 Night view of additions showing large opening wall to north-facing court

4 New zinc-lined bathroom with concrete and teak floor

5 Looking west from old building to new pavilion via new walkway

6 Internal view of new long pavilion with scissor trusses

7 Entry between new pavilions

Photography: Craigee Lee

SWATT HOUSE

Lafayette, California, USA

Swatt Architects

2

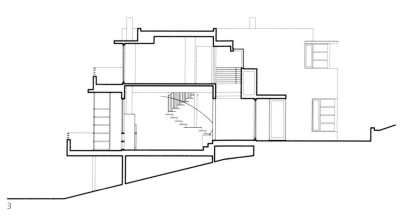

3

4

Opposite:
North elevation from pool patio

2   Exterior detail

3   Section

4   View of house from carport

5   Living/dining room

Photography: JD Peterson (1,3); Indivar Sivanathan (2);
Russell Abraham (4)

5

6

7

8

9

10

6   View from living/dining room
7   Entry spine with skylight above
8   Kitchen and breakfast areas
9   View of kitchen area from dining room
10 Upper-level stair railing detail

Photography: Russell Abraham (6,8,9); JD Peterson (7,10)

SWEET POND

Lunenburg, Nova Scotia, Canada

Diamond and Schmitt Architects Incorporated

2

3

Opposite:
View from inlet

2 Living room

3 Summer pavilion

4 Kitchen

5 Verandah

Photography: Steven Evans

5

THE BUTCHER RANCH

Gonzales County, Texas, USA

Michael G. Imber, Architect

2

1

3

1 House sited on prairie landscape

2 South side of house with sleeping porch

3 Sleeping porch

4 Section

5 Kitchen recess into shed

6 Living room toward fireplace

7 Stair hall at entry foyer

Photography: Paul Bardagjy

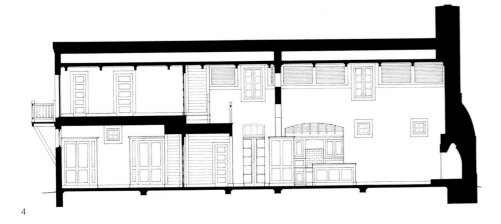

4

6

5

7

THE HAVEN

Upper Brookfield, Queensland, Australia

Paul Uhlmann Architects

Opposite:
Driveway view

2 Courtyard prior to landscaping

3 View of north elevation

4 North elevation

Photography: Matt Kennedy

2

3

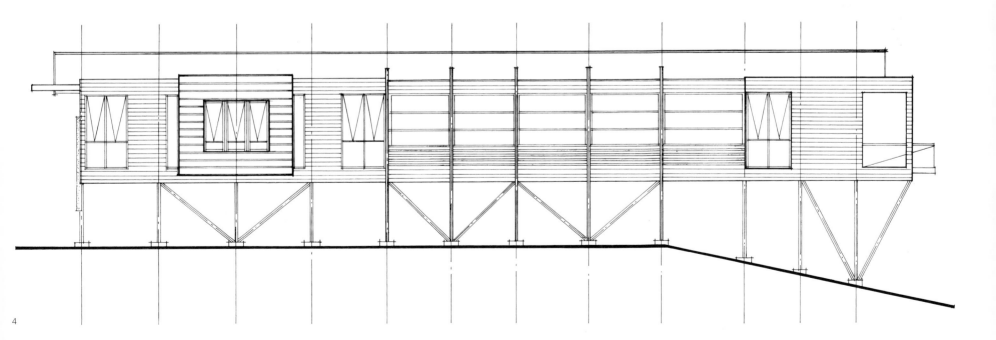

4

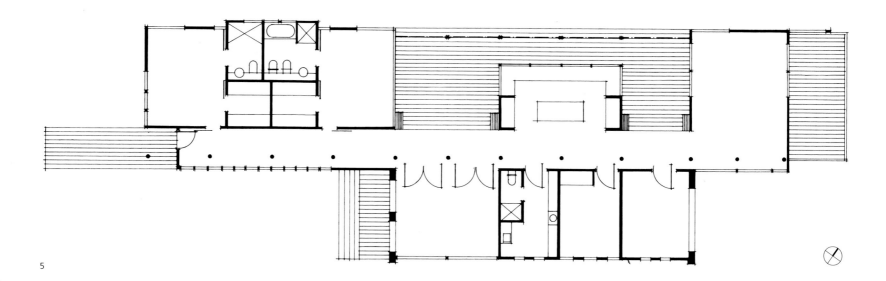

5

6

7

8

9

5 Floor plan
6 View to lounge
7 Outdoor dining
8 Outdoor living
9 Kitchen

Photography: Matt Kennedy

THE POINT HOUSE

Montana, USA

Bohlin Cywinski Jackson

2

3

Opposite:
Glassy side of building from southeast

2 East elevation nestled into rock

3 Main entry features Cor-ten steel siding panels and a custom cedar bench

4 West elevation with cantilevered deck

Photography: Dan Bibb (1,2); Nic Lehoux (3,4)

4

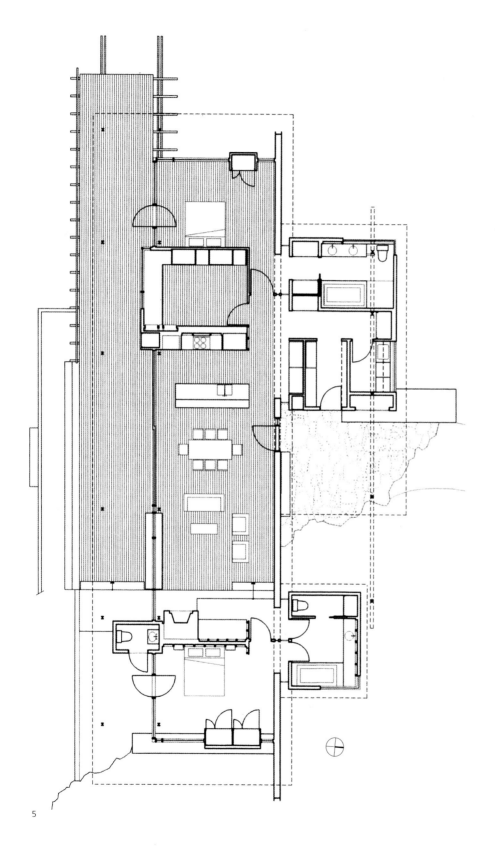

5

6

7

5   Floor plan

6   Living and dining areas look toward lake

7   East bedroom nestles into a rock spine

8   West bedroom with views to lake

9   East bathroom

10 Main hall, looking toward kitchen

Photography: Nic Lehoux

8

9

10

THE RED HOUSE

Oslo, Norway

Jarmund / Vigsnæs AS Architects

1

1 View from river valley
2 North façade
3 South façade
4 Living room viewed from terrace
5 Terrace, looking north

Photography: Nils Petter Dale

3

5

The Red House **269**

THE WATER HOUSE

Sydney, New South Wales, Australia

Dale Jones-Evans Pty Ltd

1

2

4

1 Street view of traditional restored façade and attic dormer window alterations

2 View from within pool across stone terrace to rear of glass-and-steel façade

3 Under suspended stair looking across black pebbled pool and copper-tubed fountain

4 Glazed transparent bathroom with suspended mirror cabinets and honed marble sinks

Photography: Paul Gosney

3

5

6

7

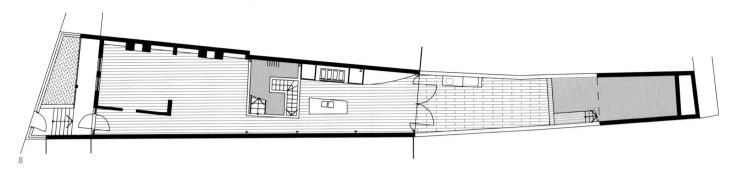

Photography: Paul Gosney

TIVOLI ROAD RESIDENCE

Melbourne, Victoria, Australia

Jan Manton Design Architecture

1

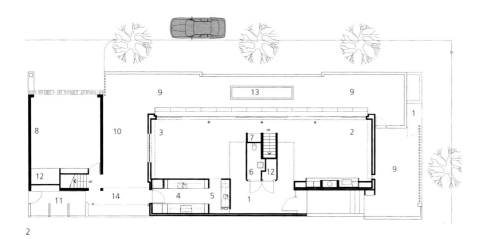

1 Entry	8 Garage	15 Bedrooms
2 Sitting room	9 Garden	16 Study
3 Dining room	10 Herb garden	17 Bathroom
4 Kitchen	11 Service	18 Laundry
5 Bar	12 Storage	19 Window seat
6 Powder room	13 Pond	20 Barbeque patio
7 Music	14 Covered access	

2

3

4

5

1 Tivoli Road view

2 Ground floor plan

3 First floor plan

4 Galley kitchen with bar at end

5 Sitting room

Photography: Earl Carter

Tivoli Road Residence **275**

6

7

8

9

Photography: Earl Carter

10

TONN RESIDENCE

Dash Point, Washington, USA

Anderson Anderson Architecture

1

2

3

1 West facing view deck

2 Model view, west elevation

3 East elevation detail, and southeast facing rooftop light monitor

4 Detail view of south elevation

5 Curved steel and maple open stair from main level to master bedroom

6 South elevation

Photography: courtesy Anderson Anderson Architecture

5

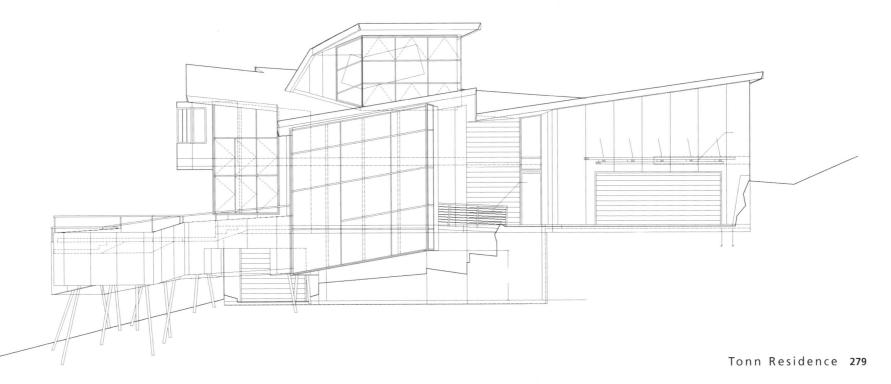

6

TREE HOUSE, STUDIO – PAVILION

Palm Beach, New South Wales, Australia

Dawson Brown Architecture

1

2

3

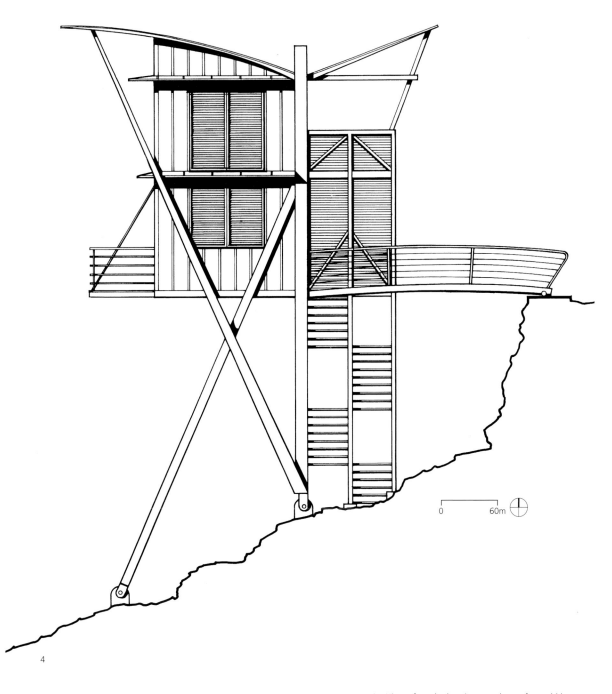

0   60m

1   View of north elevation, tree house from old house

2   Tree house from connecting bridge

3   Tree house from lower bedroom level, north elevation

4   North elevation

5   Tree house studio interior

6   Original house, new kitchen

Photography: Rob Brown

TUGUN TOWERHOUSE

Queensland, Australia

Paul Uhlmann Architects

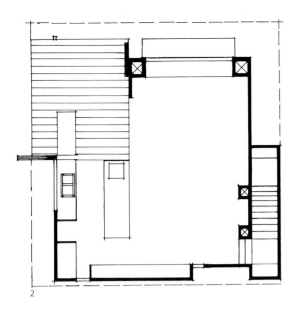

2

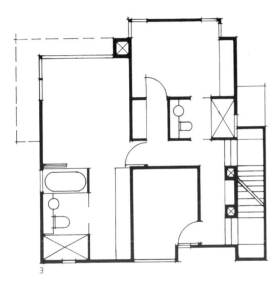

3

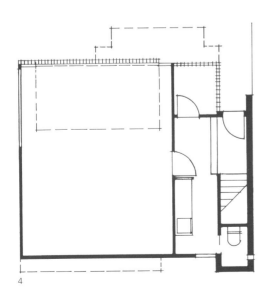

4

Opposite:

Night view

2   Second floor plan

3   First floor plan

4   Ground floor plan

5   View from southeast

Photography: David Sandison

5

8

Photography: David Sandison

9

VICTORIA PARK HOUSE

Singapore

SCDA Architects Pte Ltd

Opposite:
Front of house at dusk

2 Northwest view of living pavilion

3 Plan embraces a central courtyard with swimming pool

4 Raised terrace is tucked against rear slope

Photography: Albert Lim

2

3

4

Victoria Park House **287**

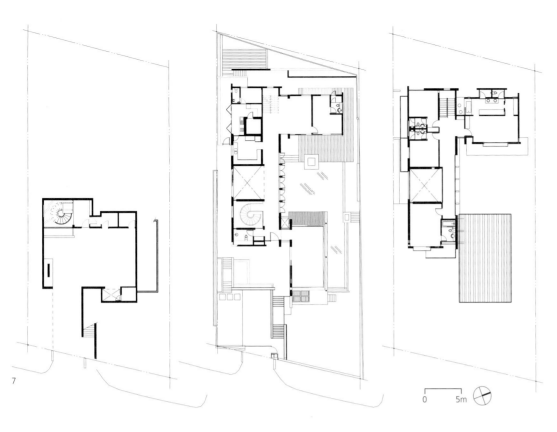

7

0   5m

8

5 Swimming pool wraps around living pavilion

6 View of living room looking toward pool

7 Floor plans

8 Living room incorporates a shallow
   monopitch aluminum roof

Photography: Albert Lim

Victoria Park House **289**

VILLA FUJII

Kitasaku, Nagano, Japan

Motomu Uno + Keizo Ikemura / Phase Associates

2

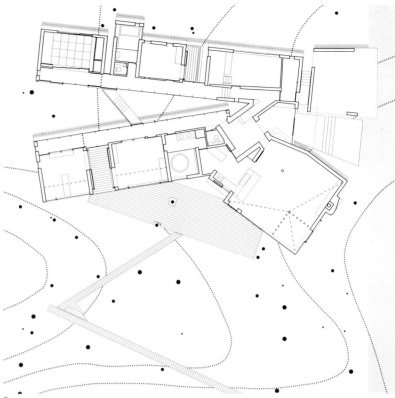

3

Opposite:
   Interior view of party space

2   Boardwalk extends toward front deck

3   Floor plan

4   Field garden

Photography: Nobuaki Nakagawa

4

6

5 Corridor, connection with rear wing

6 Japanese tatami room

7 Wooden bath, open to forest

8 View of entry space

Photography: Nobuaki Nakagawa

5

7

8

WARATAH BAY HOUSE

Walkerville/Waratah Bay, Victoria, Australia

Holan Joubert Architects

Opposite:

  Interior second level, view from kitchen

2 Exterior, northwest view at night

3 Exterior, southwest view at night

4 Section

5 Exterior, north view

Photography: Peter Hyatt

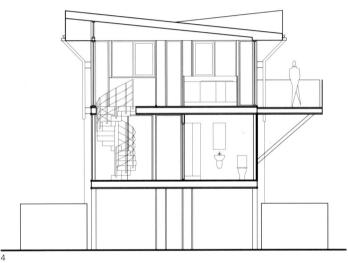

WEATHERING STEEL HOUSE

Toronto, Ontario, Canada

Shim-Sutcliffe Architects

2

Opposite:
   Street elevation

2   View of reflecting pool from living space inside

3   Swimming pool and back elevation

Photography: James Dow

3

4

5

6

0   10ft

7

4   Circulation layer showing stair to second floor
     and bridge to master bedroom
5   View of entry, looking up stair to second floor
6   First floor plan
7   Living room
8   Inverted bay window on second floor

Photography: James Dow

8

WEBSTER RESIDENCE

Venice, California, USA

Steven Ehrlich Architects

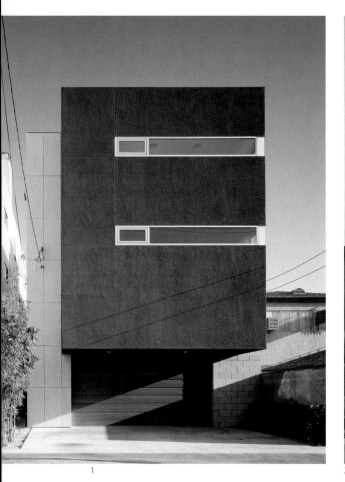

1

2

3

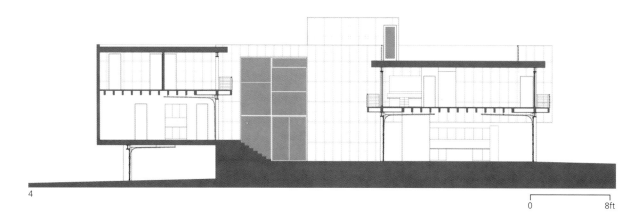

4

0   8ft

Photography: fotoworks: Benny Chan

WILLIAMS RESIDENCE

Marion, Virginia, USA

Kamal Amin Associates

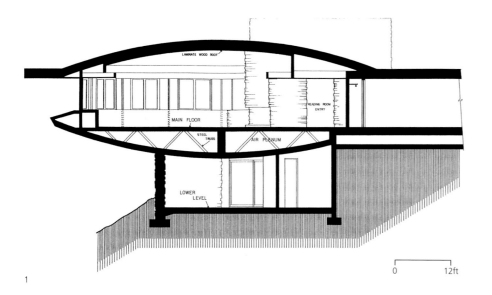

Photography: Kamal Amin

5

7

6

9

8

WILLIERS HOUSE

Tampa, Florida, USA

John Howey & Associates

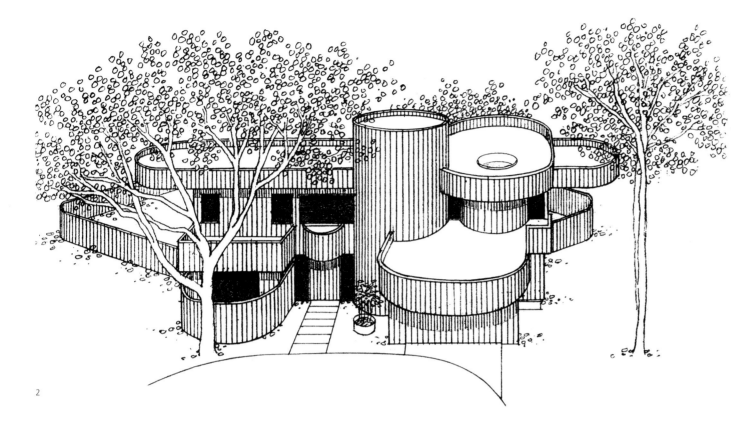

2

Opposite:

    View looking west

2 Aerial view of front

3 View looking east

4 Entry view at oak tree

Photography: George Cott (Opposite);
Steven Brooke (3,4)

3

4

6

0   15m

7

8

WILSON HOUSE

Marlborough Sounds, New Zealand

John Daish Architects & Kebbell Daish

1

2

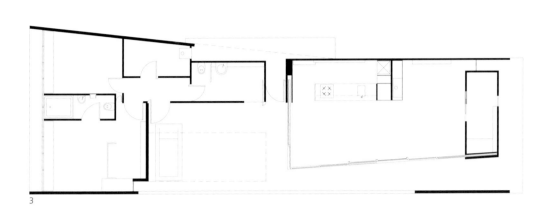

3

4

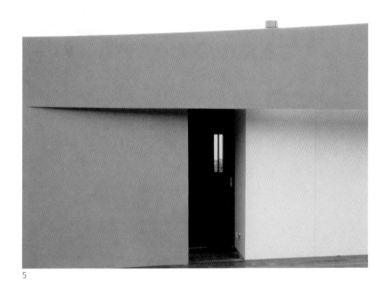

5

6

7

1 View from southeast

2 View from north

3 Floor plan

4 Courtyard and bath

5 Main entrance

6 View from east

7 Arrival view

Photography: Jono Rotman (1,2);
Sarah Connor (4–7)

WINDY HILL

Northern Mississippi, USA

Ken Tate Architect

Opposite:

View recalls a Gertrude Jekyl and Sir Edwin Lutyens collaboration

2 Aerial view showing symbiotic relationship between architecture and gardens

3 Rouge Texas limestone rubble walls contrast with pristine massing and lush landscaping

4 Changes in level and rich natural materials help create a beautiful pool environment

Photography: Gordon Beall (Opposite,4); Carlos Studio (2); Richard Felber (3)

2

3

4

5

6

5   Dovecoat is focal point for rose garden, seen here from adjoining courtyard

6   Local Mennonites hand-built the rear timber-frame porch first in a nearby cornfield

7   Complex cabinetry in the kitchen was built by Mennonite master carpenter, Kevin Yoder

8   Scored plaster entry walls rise dramatically into a groin-vaulted trompe l'oeil sky

9   Breakfast room was made in England, brought over, installed, and then 'limed'

Photography: Richard Felber (5); Gordon Beall (6–9)

7

8

WINGS

Escondido, California, USA

Norm Applebaum AIA, Architect

1 Patio
2 Bedroom 1
3 Bedroom 2
4 Garage
5 Office
6 Family room
7 Outdoor dining
8 Kitchen
9 Dining
10 Patio
11 Living room
12 Library
13 Master bedroom
14 Master bath
15 Patio
16 Pool
17 Patio
18 Guest house
19 Guest bedroom 1
20 Patio
21 Guest bedroom 2

FLOOR PLAN

Opposite:

Entry exterior at dusk

2 Floor plan

3 Early morning exterior; living room cantilevers over hillside

4 Living room ceiling appears to float above, separated by the clerestory

5 Entry doors, featuring a leaded glass composition, illustrate a bird in flight

Photography: Kim Brun (1,3,4); Norm Applebaum (5)

3

4

5

WOOD RESIDENCE

Hillsborough, California, USA

House + House Architects
Brukoff Design Associates, Interiors

Opposite:
Rear façade at dusk

2 Exterior view from north

3 Front façade

4 Main floor plan

Photography: Tom Rider

2

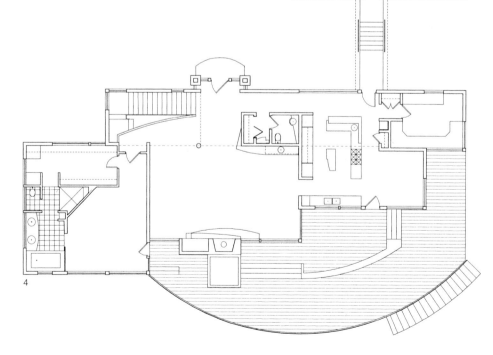

4

3

Photography: Tom Rider

5

7

6

8

9

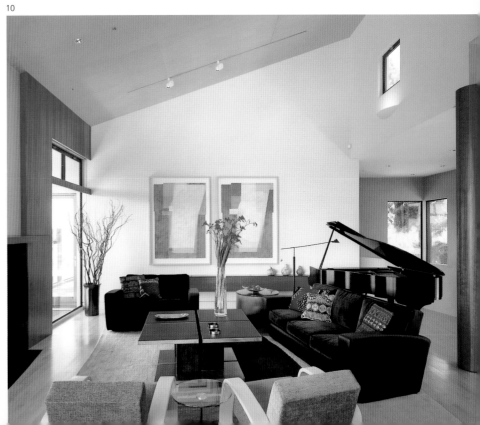

10

WOODS DRIVE RESIDENCE

Los Angeles, California, USA

Aleks Istanbullu Architects

2

3

Opposite:
Dramatic entry carries design themes from exterior to interior

2 Minimalist kitchen opens to exterior and upstairs

3 Curved wall doubles as art display space

4 Floor plan

Photography: Grant Mudford

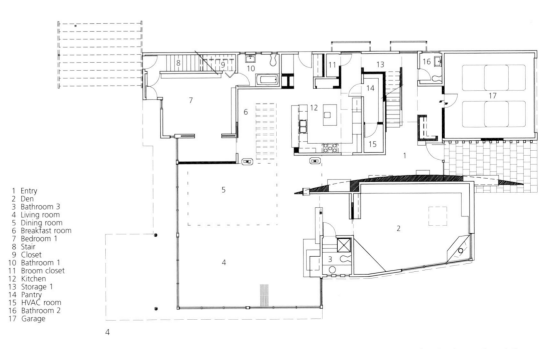

1 Entry
2 Den
3 Bathroom 3
4 Living room
5 Dining room
6 Breakfast room
7 Bedroom 1
8 Stair
9 Closet
10 Bathroom 1
11 Broom closet
12 Kitchen
13 Storage 1
14 Pantry
15 HVAC room
16 Bathroom 2
17 Garage

4

5 Skylights, light wells, and windows maintain connection to outdoors

6 Master bath is physically and visually accessible

7 Second-floor landing is kept spare with glass railings

8 Windows on all sides connect indoors with views of city

Photography: Grant Mudford

8

WOOLLAHRA RESIDENCE

Woollahra, New South Wales, Australia

Alexander Tzannes Associates

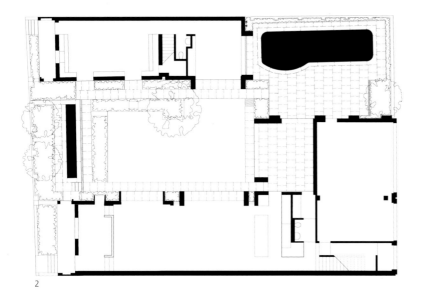

2

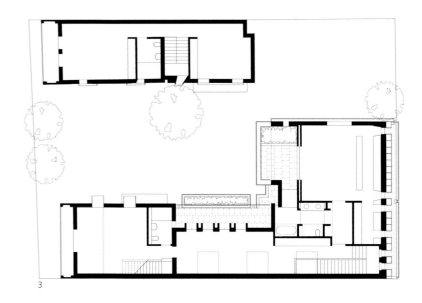

3

4

5

Opposite:
View through to courtyard

2 Ground floor plan

3 Upper floor plan

4 Living and dining area

5 Ensuite to main bedroom

Photographer: Bart Maiorana

6

8

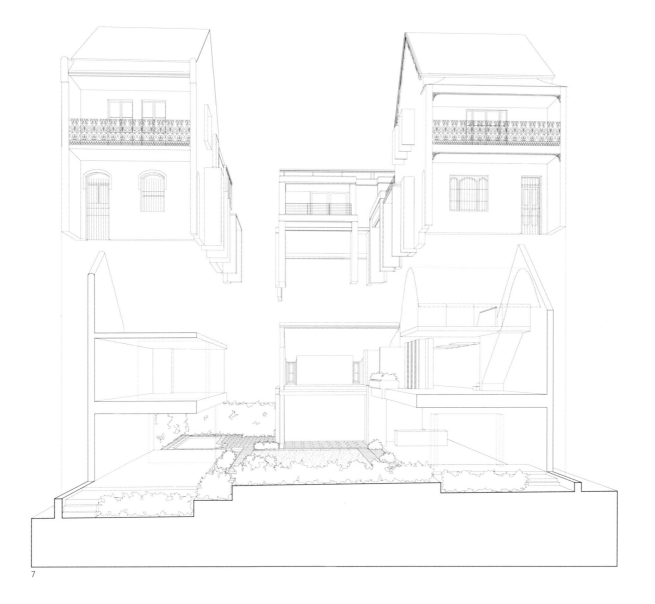

7

6 View from street

7 Exploded perspective

8&10 Courtyard views

9 Bedroom and loggia

11 View from guest wing

Photographer: Bart Maiorana

9

10

11

YELLOW VILLA

Palanga, Lithuania

Vilius Ir Partneriai: Vilius Adomavicius and Vida Vysniauskiene

1

2

3

1 South elevation
2 Terrace view
3 Courtyard
4 Bathroom
5 Staircase
6 Living room
7 Master bedroom

Photography: Raimondas Urbakavicius

4

5

6

7

20–22 Daleham Mews

London, UK
bere:architects

House area: 2540 square feet/235 square meters
Site area: 1120 square feet/104 square meters
Materials: brick, steel, glass, timber

The brief was for a well-known car designer, formerly with the German manufacturer Audi, but now heading an independent consultancy with an international client base. The cost of construction was approximately £300,000. Because of the nature of the site, which was a restricted triangular shape, and the strictly residential usage of the surrounding buildings, great constraints were imposed on the scheme, which nevertheless had to provide the client with the living accommodation and the workspace he needed.

The mews house was rebuilt to accommodate a rooftop studio and space for a young family below. The exterior complies with the requirements of the planners with an elevation that replicates the original proportions and features. The new design includes a graceful staircase finished in polished plaster and a curved, all-glass studio opening onto a roof garden. Negotiations with English Heritage, the local planning authority, and local residents resulted in the recommendation and approval of a scheme that overturns many of the restrictions imposed upon the site and has provided a valuable extra floor and garden for the client.

3 Aberdeen Lane

London, UK
Azman Owens Architects

House area: 2570 square feet/239 square meters
Site area: 4120 square feet/383 square meters
Materials: fair-faced insitu concrete (internal and external walls), timber-framed doors and windows, timber shutters, glass screens, limestone floors (ground floor), timber floor (first floor)

This new-build house is located on an unadopted lane dominated by workshops, studios, and light industrial sheds. The site is bordered by a detached house on the west side, terraced mews houses on the east side, and a garden wall at the rear. There already was planning permission for two mews houses positioned to align with the adjacent mews houses. The planners were keen to adhere to the existing planning permission, particularly in relation to the orientation of the proposed houses. This would have resulted in a north-facing garden. We decided to submit a planning application proposing the building in its current position.

The decision to face the house inwards to create a courtyard was followed by a series of decisions that led to the choice of materials and method of construction. It was decided that north and south walls to the house (the walls facing the lane and the house at the rear) would be treated as solid without many openings, in order to maintain a definitive edge to the lane and avoid overlooking. The other instrumental parameter was the depth of the mews house at the east side of the site. With these two critical decisions, the house was designed as two interlocking cubes of internally and externally exposed reinforced concrete walls. The choice of concrete was driven by the desired solidness of the north and south walls. The house was designed like a doll's house with a west-facing 'courtyard' façade left transparent with large panes of glass in timber framing. Timber louvers are installed at first-floor level for a degree of privacy. The structure is a series of insitu concrete planes; horizontal flat slabs with double cantilever overhangs and planar walls with reinforced concrete external cavity walls.

511 House

Pacific Palisades, California, USA
Kanner Architects

House area: 3200 square feet/300 square meters
Site area: 7200 square feet/670 square meters

The challenge in the design of the 511 House was to create a bright, modern, Southern California home able to embrace the outdoors. Blurring the line between inside and outside was of the highest priority. To do this, the main body of the two-story plan was pushed to the north side of the standard tennis court-sized lot. A wide patio extends to the south off the lower level and it is this generous setback that enables the southern light to penetrate the house. Large sliding glass doors pull away, allowing the inside to merge with the outside.

The modernist esthetic is inspired by nearby houses by Richard Neutra and Charles and Ray Eames. However, it is a house of its time and is completely unique as its textures, materials and fenestrations make a personal statement. There is a metaphorical juxtaposition of rough to smooth materials (scratch-coat plaster versus smooth mosaic tile) that recalls the relationship of the ocean to the mountains. Landscaping is critical to the scheme as it is the key to creating a private world. Timber bamboo, black bamboo, and ficus hedges are placed in front of horizontally slatted cedar fencing, screening neighboring homes. Gravel paths at the drip line and a large lawn surround to the south and west. At the street, a V-shaped specimen palm layers the front façade, while bands of Japanese grass, gravel and lawn graphically recall the scoring pattern in the front yard hardscape.

The 511 House is about Southern California living—inside/out. The plan, section and site plan are of greatest importance. How can a typical lot be utilized to make it seem larger and more open? Solving the planning problems in a unique way allows the design of the envelope to become secondary. This is a house about lifestyle, not just another home with a contemporary façade.

A Cabin in the Woods

Scientists Cliffs, Maryland, USA
Good Architecture

House area: 3500 square feet/325 square meters
Site area: 30,000 square feet/2787 square meters
Materials: wood-frame construction with painted gypsum board (interior); log slab, vertical board-and-batten (exterior)

In 1935, G. Flippo Gravatt and his wife, both forest pathologists in the Department of Agriculture, purchased 238 wooded acres (96 hectares) on a high cliff overlooking the Chesapeake Bay in Calvert County, Maryland. This site was used to establish a summer colony of scientists and was named Scientists Cliffs. Today there are 200 houses, a community house, tennis courts, swimming pool, maintenance office, dedicated parkland, and community vegetable gardens.

The architecture of Scientists Cliffs developed as tiny 600-square-foot (56-square-meter), iconic log cabins, many of which were originally constructed of solid chestnut logs that weathered to a beautiful reddish-brown. Today, only a few of the early cabins remain intact with their original chestnut logs—most have been insensitively altered and enlarged. Although the community maintains written design guidelines and a design review process, later development within the community has tended to be architecturally arbitrary, out of scale and character, and of mediocre or poor design quality.

The client's program called for a retirement home with one-floor living on the main level, and guest accommodation, a family crafts room, and an office on the lower level. The new house was designed as a series of four small, connected cabins each about the size of an original Scientists Cliffs cabin. Clad in a combination of log slab and vertical board-and-batten siding, our project attempts to demonstrate that current living patterns and the desire for significantly larger houses that come with full-time residency can be accommodated within architectural forms that are compatible in scale, proportion, massing, and materials that appropriately reinforce the history and the original idea of Scientists Cliffs.

A House in the Country

Aconcagua Valley, Chile
Germán del Sol, Architect

House area: 8500 square feet/790 square meters
Site area: 70 acres/28 hectares
Materials: concrete, native timbers

This large family country home in the Aconcagua Valley, Chile, was built on a 70-acre (28-hectare) grassland site. The floor level of the house is raised 5 feet (1.5 meters) above the ground to capture sunlight and distant views, while retaining the privacy of the patios, the big open spaces associated with country life. Rough, low-maintenance materials have been used throughout the indoor and outdoor living areas to provide maximum comfort. A dispersed and crisscrossed floor plan extends the façade's length and forms long, shaded terraces around the house. Rooms have been designed with flexibility in mind, allowing for changes in use as the family's needs change.

Andrew Road House

Singapore
SCDA Architects Pte Ltd

House area: 14,610 square feet/1357 square meters
Site area: 22,830 square feet/2121 square meters

The Andrew Road House consists of three blocks on a rectangular site that slopes approximately 13 feet (4 meters) from east to west.

The first block is the single-story reception pavilion that is open on all four sides. This transparent space is revealed upon passing through an opening in a stone wall, which is located across the pedestrian entrance axis. Having arrived at the center, one turns abruptly to the right and encounters the largest of the three blocks, containing the principal living and dining areas, the master bedroom and the secondary bedrooms. This block is entered across a bridge and through a thick screen wall so the experience of the interior is again delayed and the sense of anticipation heightened. The entrance pavilion, located at the southern end, is a 10-foot-high (3-meter) circular 'lantern' constructed of timber, and lined with a woven steel fabric. This lantern is lit from within and is the visual focus of the pavilion.

The third block overlooks the swimming pool and a waterfall. This is the lowest area of the site and although two stories high, its roof is at the same level as the single-story entrance pavilion. It serves as an entertainment and guest suite and is clad with a permeable metal screen. A sub-basement vehicle court with parking for four cars is located beneath the entrance pavilion.

Berty House

East Hampton, New York, USA
Alfredo De Vido Associates

House area: 5800 square feet/539 square meters
Site area: 1.7 acres/0.7 hectares

The clients wanted a house for either weekend or full-time use in an exurban area. They both admired the vernacular architecture of the area and so the resulting building used wood as its main building material. The approach to the house is marked by a series of pools and a kinetic sculpture designed by the architect. The landscape around the building is handsome and features a number of gardens planned by the owners. Bridges provide points of entry to the house over the gardens.

As the owners enjoy entertaining, the main floor contains a space large enough to hold 100 for a sit-down dinner. A fireplace is the focal point of one end of the room and at the other there is an 'art wall' to hold changing displays of paintings and sculpture. Lighting is built in and has the capability of varying its levels.

The main downstairs space is a media center and family room. Off this space is a workroom which is accessible to a greenhouse above. The greenhouse is another sitting area, which is mainly built of glass, is sunny, and filled with plants. This room can also be reached from the living room via a bridge. Nearby are decks with trellis, pleasant for outdoor dining in fine weather and close to the vegetable and flower gardens. Overhangs and brise soleil regulate the strong summer sun while admitting beneficial winter sun to the building. An important consideration in the planning was thermal efficiency and syphonic cooling which is provided for with high, operable skylights and low intakes.

Brick Bay Pavilion

Brick Bay, Warkworth, New Zealand
Noel Lane Architects

House area: 700 square feet/65 square meters
Site area: 200 acres/81 hectares
Materials: Moleanos stone (cabinetry, column cladding, bathroom flooring); blonded pine (ceiling); blonded ash (flooring); fiberglass plywood (roof); anodized aluminum (window/door joinery)

The Brick Bay Guest House strives to be as minimal an enclosure as possible without compromising its habitability, and provides serviced overnight accommodation for two guests. The building stands in a rural, coastal landscape, like an umbrella on a deck. It provides occupants, at the least, basic shelter from sun and rain. The interior is contained, or not, by sliding glass walls and automatic blinds assuring its adaptability to individual requirements in response to varying internal or external conditions. The palette of materials used is minimal. These are utilized continuously within and without, reinforcing the transparency of the architecture in the landscape.

Burraworrin Residence

Flinders, Victoria, Australia
Gregory Burgess Architects

House area: 7000 square feet/650 square meters
Materials: standard timber-framed construction, with exposed galvanized steel elements

The Burraworrin (aboriginal word for 'magpie') Residence is located about 1300 feet (400 meters) from a coastal road. The property is relatively flat, with an undulating landscape of pasture grass and full exposure to the weather; the house follows the landscape, resulting in minimal exposure from the road.

The house is designed to accommodate four related families. It is sited to maximize the full potential of solar gain and provide protection against the coastal winds. The house opens to the north where grassed terraces, a swimming pool and sundeck are protected from the southwest winds. Living spaces are interconnected and open. Radiating from the kitchen, open living areas incorporate panoramic views to each other and the views outside. The breakfast area overlooks a protected terrace, barbeque area and swimming pool. The sunken fire pit is contained and engulfed by the living room. Master bedrooms are accessed away from living spaces and are close to the children's area. The children's area includes bedrooms, bath, and rumpus rooms, which open to the courtyard for play.

The building was designed to be energy-efficient in the exposed conditions, to maximize solar gain and protection against prevailing winds. North lighting (protected by external shading systems), and broad shaded verandas provide passive solar protection. Solar hydronic heating and sweep fans are used for low-energy climate maintenance, and the swimming pool is heated by solar hot water. Views of the surrounding coastline can be seen from all rooms within the house, and the lookout atop the house affords 360-degree views of the surrounding coastal, bay and island scenery.

Canal House

Venice, California, USA
Sander Architects

House area: 2200 square feet/204 square meters
Site area: 2520 square feet/234 square meters

The Canal House is composed of three cubes: one raised at the street as a studio, and two together at the canalside as the residence. In its concept and execution, the house is informed by two ideas, one embracing the possibility of the poetic, the other a more specific kind of material formation:

Inference: in its separate masses, the house sets up an opposition between studio and residence: work/live, sky/earth, idea/body. An attempt is made to keep this discussion covert and nuanced rather than overt. The studio is a raised, pure space, marked by horizontal steel fins providing indirect light through three transparent walls. By contrast, the residence might be considered solidly grounded, mostly opaque, somewhat inward-looking. As the studio might further take on aspects of thought, connoted by simplicity and purity of form, the residence is all body; stepped, winding, turning.

Tectonics: within both volumes, surfaces have been folded, warped, wrapped, and while there are few interior walls per se, space is divided sufficiently, both horizontally and vertically, to allow place and hierarchy. A pseudo mobius strip of 1-inch sanded (horizontal) acrylic forms a divider/wall/handrail, which wraps around and through the upper house level, encircling the central atrium. This wall starts as four ribbons, each 2 feet tall, then becomes two (handrail), then one (guardrail fill), passing beneath itself at the origin. Stair treads are formed from folded half-inch steel plate, as is the fireplace mantle/facing/hearth. The kitchen island is cantilevered sheets of Wavecore Panelite, 'folded' into an L-section. Parachute nylon wraps the first floor living and dining areas.

Casa del Sol Fernández

La Dehesa, Santiago, Chile
Germán del Sol, Architect

House area: 3360 square feet/312 square meters
Site area: 15,000 square feet/1394 square meters
Materials: concrete, native timbers

This family home project is founded in ideas shared with the architect's brother, his wife, and their sons. In this house, one is invited to slow down, attracted by the continuous movement of light that washes rough zigzag walls in ever-changing forms; changes of form and movement that come and go to nowhere, like ocean waves or fire flames.

The unexpected is always present in the house, to be perceived with some sense of humor, as an invitation to be children again, always attracted by what happens outside the self. The house is also to be enjoyed by wandering inside and outside as if in a never-ending journey. There is neither a highlight nor a culmination of its experience. The architecture attempts to reunite the inner differences always present in a family, to provide the option of solitude or family interaction. Thus, it creates a destination where they all feel at home.

This house, as many works of architecture, is made out of right and wrong guesses, because bad ideas help to find the good ones. This house was built with the intention to be able to see in the apparent flaws, the hidden quality of things that accompany us during life. Things in which beauty may be found, when one sets them free to be what they are, and not what they are supposed to be. The house is obviously designed from the inside out.

Castle Creek Lodge

Aspen, Colorado, USA
42|40 Architecture Inc, formerly Urban Design Group/Denver and Chicago

House area: (including garage and caretaker's quarters attached by a log loggia, two-story horse barn [unbuilt]) 14,000 square feet/1300 square meters
Materials: concrete foundations, traditional bearing log construction up to sills of second floor, wood frame above with pre-engineered wood trusses at roof; stone, log, shingle, stained concrete, antique heart pine floors, ceilings and interior trim

Designed in the eclectic tradition of National Parks-style lodges, this large private residence is both formally planned, yet casually outfitted. With a stone, log and shingle-style exterior, the rooms are organized around a visual axis terminating at the 13,500-foot (4115-meter) peak of Mt. Hayden.

Comprising approximately 10,000 square feet of living space (930 square meters), the house includes five bedrooms, a caretaker/guesthouse, and several private balconies and covered patios, giving a sense of vast, yet cozy spaces for quality family living. The house features 22-foot (6.7-meter) cathedral ceilings and floor-to-ceiling windows that bring the surrounding stunning landscape indoors. An imposing two-story totem pole, representing the eternal nature of family, resides in the entry hall, setting the theme for the eclectic décor throughout. Unique woodwork details give each room its own personality, and some surprises, such as a 'secret' passage off the library, reinforce the quirky atmosphere of the home. The lighting was specially designed to re-create turn-of-the-century lantern lighting, with the use of lamps, wall sconces and chandeliers, but with modern touches such as concealed halogen lights.

Stained concrete floors, the extensive use of antique heart pine, colorful exterior elements and a dramatic log entry porch are some of the contemporary touches that complement the subtle blend of Cowboy Arts and Crafts and traditional log design.

CH House

La Garriga, Barcelona, Spain
BAAS

The building is conceived as an abstract, out-of-context object, with few material references, in the manner of a box that has simply been deposited on the surface of the lawn, highly hermetic and opaque in its longitudinal façades—a necessary defence from the overwhelming proximity of the neighbors.

The interior is organized around the nucleus of the entrance vestibule and a courtyard. This central band separates the rooms of non-continuous use (children's bedrooms and guest bedrooms), from the rest of the house, which is conceived as a single fluid and continuous space, subtly arranged around two pieces of furniture that organize the space into three parallel centerlines. The central one is occupied by the living room and transition spaces between it and the entrance vestibule. In turn, the dining room is separate from the living room and acts as a transition piece between it and the kitchen.

In the centerline along the south façade, there is a sequence of related spaces. The ensuite bathroom of the master bedroom is formalized into a wooden volume, organizing this sector of the home and separating the bedroom area that opens fully on to the west façade, from the dressing room that opens on to the interior courtyard. The natural lighting of the bathroom is achieved through a skylight that occupies the entire shower area and a shift in the façade that allows the light to penetrate tangentially. This lateral façade is organized around the opening corresponding to the master bedroom, thus emphasising its opacity. The wall of the bath is shifted in order to integrate the bathroom into the garden and results in angled openings that are concealed from the gaze of the neighbors. On the front façade, this same abstract-leaning purpose of the lateral enclosure is reproduced, in an effort to open the principal rooms to the outside. The entire house has been built from only two materials, white and wood, with no distinction between interior and exterior.

Concrete Poll House

Perth, Western Australia, Australia
Gary Marinko Architects

House area: 5382 square feet/500 square meters
Site area: 15,070 square feet/1400 square meters
Materials: insulated tilt-up concrete, glazed bricks, common bricks with concrete dado finish, Zincalume metal sheets in a Custom Orb profile, fiberglass sheets in a 'supa six' profile, pressed galvanized iron louvers with a powder-coated finish, painted plasterboard, anodized aluminum windows, Zebrano veneered hollow-core doors, Sika 325 polyurethane on a concrete slab floor

On a sloping suburban site, we were asked to design two residences; one for the clients and their visiting children's families, the other a flat for the client's mother. In addition, it was requested that passive means be utilized to maintain a comfortable internal environment and all the buildings had to be fully wheelchair-accessible. This necessitated the levelling of the site to gain an appropriate compromise between the vehicular access from both the street and right of way. The result was a building that was below the level of its neighbors. Access to light through the walls along these boundaries was limited.

The buildings are oriented toward the north for optimum solar gain and around a series of courtyards from which all the internal rooms gain light. Supplementing this are large louvered skylights. At night, light is projected onto the walls; in the main spaces the fiberglass volumes of the kitchen glow and appear as a solid form of light; there are no lights in the ceiling. The major circulation routes are around the edges of the building. The west hall is a private route to the master bedroom, retreat, and study; the east hall is the public route past the guest room, meals area and into the living and dining spaces. Once past the enclosure of the bedrooms, one can always see the full extent of the house, either through the courtyards or past the freestanding fiberglass volumes of the kitchen. The living spaces of the flat are oriented towards its own north-facing courtyard.

To aid the passive regulation of temperature within the house, a large volume of thermal mass was incorporated within the walls. The external shading ensures that the walls have maximum exposure to sunlight in winter, but are free of the sun in the summer. These walls are site-poured, pre-cast concrete panels, which are a combination of structure, insulation, and cladding, poured in stages and lifted into place after curing.

Connecticut Residence

Connecticut, USA
Elliott + Associates Architects

House area: 8775 square feet/815 square meters

We had three conceptual goals. We wanted to create a house whose very existence is inspired by a modern and African art collection. It was to be a place where the interior and exterior embrace in appreciation of one another. It was our intent to appreciate classic modernism. There are no trends, no fashion, no tricks. At the outset, our intention was to enhance and develop the interior/exterior relationships. The 10-foot-high (3-meter) steel-and-glass curtain wall creates the envelope of the structure without imposing spatial boundaries. The relationship between man and nature is a 1-inch separation physically and zero visually. The window mullions become delicate picture frames outlining nature beyond. In this house, nature becomes art.

The structure is perched atop a hill overlooking an Atlantic Ocean tributary with natural stone outcroppings defining the perimeter and its wetlands. The glass wall along the northeast elevation provides a stunning view into the treetops creating the sensation of being suspended between the 70-foot-tall (21-meter) trees. This is a house where moods change by day and night; when the trees are green or bare or covered with snow or softened by fog. This house is a declaration of how beautiful man and nature can be in harmony. Modern architecture and nature are beautiful together.

The primary goal for the interior architecture is to create surroundings that complement and enhance the display of modern art and African sculpture. Special consideration was given to the African sculpture with the use of polished black granite slabs that visually absorb their bases and highlight the shapes with pure white backgrounds.

Awards include: American Institute of Architects, National Honor Award for Interiors; American Society of Interior Designers, National Interior Design Project Award.

Coromandel Bach

Coromandel, New Zealand
Crosson Clarke Architects

House area: 1378 square feet/128 square meters
Site area: 26 acres/10.4 hectares
Materials: structural members: eucalyptus Saligna cladding and joinery; Lawson cypress wall linings; Hoop pine

The house was conceived as a container sitting lightly on the land for habitation or the dream of habitation. The intention was to reinterpret the New Zealand building tradition of the crafting of wood—the expression of structure, cladding, lining and joinery in a raw and unique way. The construction is reminiscent of the 'trip' or 'rafter' dams common in the Coromandel region at the turn of last century: heavy vertical structural members supporting horizontal boarding.

The unadorned natural timber, a sustainable and renewable resource, provides a connection to nature and the natural. A simple mechanism to the deck allows the 'box' to open up on arrival, providing a stage for living, and to close down on departure, providing protection. The house has a simple, rectangular plan that sits across the contour in a patch of cleared bush in the manner of the rural shed, facing north and the view. The living room is open to the outside and the sun, a metaphorical tent or campsite, while the bunkrooms are enclosed and cool. The large fireplace allows winter occupation and the open bathroom and movable bath allows the rituals of showering and bathing to become an experience connected to nature.

This bach is an attempt to provide an environment to capture the essential spirit of the New Zealand holiday in the New Zealand landscape. ['Bach' is a typically New Zealand word that describes a weekend cottage or house, usually at the beach.]

Corum Residence

Pella, Iowa, USA
Herbert Lewis Kruse Blunck Architecture

House area: 2785 square feet/259 square meters
Site area: 4 acres/1.6 hectares
Materials: Galvalume, galvanted plate siding, woven stainless steel guardrails, aluminum windows/curtainwall, Lumasite, maple flooring, maple cabinetry, industrial chalk board

While expressing its own distinct presence on the horizon, this modest home simultaneously suggests a presence greater than itself—the rural Iowa landscape. The elemental design gestures to a rolling, pastoral vista both internally and externally. Its simple form references agricultural buildings prevalent in the central United States.

The home's spatial organization places the more public 'living' spaces in relation to the view, while sequestering the private 'bed and bath' functions deep within the metal-clad wedge— a form that, in turn, is directed toward the distant hills. Internally, the home's open plan utilizes a system of maple and acrylic shelving, an open-riser stair, and a fireplace mass to vertically organize the section and link the three levels.

D'Ottavi Residence

North Adelaide, South Australia, Australia
Studio 9 Architects

House area: 3789 square feet/352 square meters
Site area: 6039 square feet/561 square meters
Materials: internal: bianco Carrara marble, select grade quarter-cut walnut veneer, 6mm TH glass, 400 x 400mm terrazzo tiles; external: BEST bricks and pavers, Zincalume roofing

The client purchased the site with the idea to demolish the house and start again with a new substantial residence. With further examination of the property, and taking into account its well-resolved design and detailing, it was demonstrated that it was possible to satisfy the spatial requirements of the new brief through the reuse of the existing structure and with minimal building additions.

The first floor kitchen has been relocated to the building core to create a defined cantilevered bay dining area and adjacent living room. This, in addition to the relocation of the main entry stairs, opened up the living area, allowing a small study or private television room and a new guest bathroom to be included where the kitchen had been previously. The previous two-way bathroom has been converted into an ensuite following on from the dressing room of the master bedroom. The lowering of the garage floor level by approximately 12 inches (300 mm) has created a secondary, less formal living area while still retaining a two-car garage, a storeroom and a wine cellar. The upper and lower living areas and the garage have been linked with the enclosure of the existing external stair and lobby.

A new refined selection of finishes was introduced, including Carrara marble, walnut, glass and terrazzo with all major internal walls rendered and painted white. The original concrete slab was polished and remains the dominant floor finish throughout the first floor of the house. The main joinery items for the living area, the kitchen, all cupboards, sliding doors and loose joinery were designed on the idea that all unnecessary details should be removed and have minimal hardware, with the texture depth coming from the finish itself. The rear garden area is centrally accessible from the top of the internal stair; the rear and side landscaped areas have been terraced with raised planters for the herb garden. The primary upper living and sleeping areas are serviced by large protected balcony areas.

Dalwhinnie

Queenstown, New Zealand
Murray Cockburn Partnership

House area: 2706 square feet/251 square meters
Site area: 1 acre/0.4 hectare
Materials: reinforced concrete and blockwork, Butynol rubber membrane roofing with fiberglass insulation, double-glazed aluminum windows, polystyrene external wall cladding, native New Zealand timbers and oregon, Italian ceramic tiles, Glenorchy rock and slate, Resene paints, Dulux Acra-tex rendered internal/external surfaces, in-slab electric and convection wall heaters, Rinnai gas space-heater

Set high above Lake Wakatipu, in the mountains of the South Island, this luxuriously proportioned residence provides the clients with some of New Zealand's most spectacular panoramic views. The site, bounded by sheer cliffs and steeply forested falls, is situated on a rounded rocky ridge, below Mt. Ben Lomond. Its aspect is primarily south, but the house has been purpose-built to capture all the magnificent vistas from the northeast around to the southwest, including The Remarkables, Cecil Peak, Walter Peak, and the Von Valley.

The unusual design concept uses a three-level configuration, and embraces a primary circle comprising two half-circles, one smaller than the other. A central drum tower, enclosing a thick-stepped, timber spiral staircase, made from native Rimu, locks the house into the bedrock. The tower is the pivotal point for the great, cantilevered steel I-beams, which support the upper two levels of the house and the wide, sweeping, mid-level balcony. The smaller, north-facing half-circle at the mid level forms the generous, high cathedral-ceilinged hallway, with its exposed oregon beams, all-round glass windows, impressive stone pillared entrance, and heavy, old hardwood main door.

The much larger circle encompasses all three levels, with 10-foot-wide (3-meter) picture windows at the lower and mid-levels. Guest bedrooms, each with its own inspiring views and ensuite bathroom, are located on the lower level. The mid-level provides spacious, open-plan living, with a high, oregon-beamed cathedral ceiling. It includes the half-round Nook, a snuggly comfortable television viewing space. The impressive east-facing master bedroom and ensuite are also located mid-level. The upper level is known as the Eyrie, or Eagle's Nest. It is smaller and serves the double function of office, with a semi-circular window desk, a meditation/quiet-time creative space, and built-in wall-to-windows lounge. The entire residence is finished in subtle, natural hues, directly reflecting the colors in the surrounding mountains and Lake Wakatipu. Despite its apparent remoteness, the house is located only ten minutes' drive from Queenstown.

Desert Residence

Rancho Mirage, California, USA
Olson Sundberg Kundig Allen

House area: 7200 square feet/670 square meters
Site area: 1 acre/0.4 hectare
Materials: concrete, wood, plaster

This desert home is located on a ridge above an arroyo near Palm Springs. The owners wanted a house to serve as a gracious setting for living and entertaining. The surrounding desert landscape extends to the horizon with views taking in the Santa Rosa Mountains. Native desert plantings are cultivated to make a seamless transition from the site to the desert landscape. Solidity and mass, traditional desert construction concepts, are used to provide relief from the summer heat and harsh light. Windows are located under overhanging eaves or in deeply recessed openings to limit summer sun, but to allow the sun's lower winter light into the house's interior. The resulting building form, with its deep openings and voids, is sculpted in sunlight by strong light and dark shadows.

The house is designed as a series of offset colonnades, with the spaces between the walls providing the living area. The large-scale repetitive columns and beams run through the building and into the landscape, connecting the house to its environment. Inside, these columns also create architectural frames between which art is displayed. The material palette is kept simple and the colors neutral, reflecting the surrounding desert landscape. Roof planes are designed to float above the solid walls, allowing only reflected natural light to enter. Concrete is used for columns, interior wall forms and flooring. Smooth sand-colored plaster exterior walls and flat roofs connect the contemporary design to its desert precedents. Overhangs on the southern side shade floor-to-ceiling sliding doors to take advantage of the extremely pleasant winter climate.

Edgewater

Short Hills, New Jersey, USA
WESKetch Architecture

House area: 7000 square feet/650 square meters
Site area: 1.1 acre/0.4 hectare

Locating a new home in a historic suburb that abuts a lake is quite a challenge architecturally, especially when the home is meant to look as though it has always been there. The clients were living in a developer home and desired a home that portrayed their inner style while maintaining historic detail and charm.

The views to the east and north were important and creating privacy on a corner lot was imperative. An L-shaped parti resulted from the restraints of the corner lot. By addressing both streets and keeping true to the constricting setbacks, the home has windows and ventilation on two or three sides of all rooms. The effect is a home with many detailed rooms and a plan that allows the home to sprawl around the corner. This home has a sense of permanence and character that exudes warmth through its finely hand-crafted brick façade and intricately detailed eaves and window placement.

The heart and soul of the home can be found on the interior where the English Arts and Crafts era-inspired details allow the spaces to stand alone and still flow gracefully from one room to the next. The European Craftsman elements of this home are rich with detail and many famous architects such as Edwin Lutyens helped to create this building by inspiring scale, detail and use of materials. Such details include the stacked brick quoining at the front entry aligning so carefully with all horizontal lines of the façade, custom-made European-style mahogany windows, and exposed rough-sawn cedar rafter tails with hand crafted half-round copper gutters at the eaves.

Every detail was checked and rechecked to accurately portray the historic details of the past, including the hand-made clay roof tiles from France. Despite being heavily influenced by English Craftsman designs of the past, the house is overlaid with the most-up-to date, high-performance building techniques.

Equis House

La Escondida Beach, Cañete, Peru
Barclay & Crousse Architecture, Paris

House area: 1873 square feet/174 square meters
Site area: 2723 square feet/253 square meters
Materials: exposed concrete, wood, template glass, painted surfaces

We believe that to inhabit the desert, it is essential to 'domesticate' the landscape without denying or betraying it. We decided to begin the design process by imagining an abstract and plain volume whose limits are defined by building regulations. Then, during the design process, we excavated this volume, removing matter as archeologists remove sand to discover pre-Columbian ruins in this region.

This 'subtractive logic', very different from 'constructive logic', was applied to all scales of the project. The result was exterior spaces merging with interior spaces in a continuous fluid space within a precinct, where landscape and sky are each framed in different ways. The entrance patio leads to the intimate space of the house. This space extends toward the ocean with a large terrace. This terrace is conceived as an artificial beach that relates to the ocean by a long and narrow pool. The living/dining space roof is conceived as a weightless beach umbrella, anchored to the precinct. Barriers between the living/dining space and the terrace are erased by frameless glass sliding panels. An open staircase follows the natural topography and leads to the bedroom level beneath the terrace. The children's bedrooms are accessible by a patio/pergola covered by the terrace deck, and the parents' bedroom is reached at the end of the staircase, passing under the suspended pool.

The use of ochre/sand color, found also in pre-Columbian and colonial houses, prevents the building from visually aging as it gathers layers of desert dust, and reinforces the sense of unity of the excavated volume. The long distance between our office in Paris and the Peruvian site led us to rationalize the construction system, and detail work that appeared not to be essential was eliminated. We simplified the remaining details so that they could be easily built by local craftspeople.

Fire Island House

Fire Island Pines, New York, USA
Roger Hirsch, Architect, Susan Frostén, Architect, Drew Souza, Designer

House area: 1600 square feet/149 square meters
Site area: 9600 square feet/892 square meters
Materials: exterior: clear-finish cedar, cedar decking; interior: French limestone, cleft slate, natural finish maple, blackened steel

In this two-story house, a series of deft gestures in form, materials, and color make the most of an extraordinary location, bringing together patterns of light and weather with the moods and activities of summer weekends. The house sits on wood piles driven into sandy soil, several yards inland in a wind-blown wood. Access is by raised boardwalk paths that protect a fragile ecosystem. A high orange wall creates privacy for the pool while defining a simple, modern entrance path.

The main event is the northern façade, behind which the living room opens to pool and sky through double-height glazing. Inside, a deep blue 'tower' and ochre 'cube' offer views of the bay from two of the upstairs bedrooms. Views and breezes cross the house, passing through open-riser stairs under a central skylight between the tower and cube. The living room ceiling rises 20 feet (6 meters) to exposed beams, and a skylight along the tower admits a slice of sun, whose path across the floor varies seasonally. Gentle northern light fills the room.

The floors offer tactile variety while helping to integrate interior and exterior. Cool, smooth limestone in the main living space contrasts with the rugged wood deck outdoors. Cleft-finish slate lends traction in showers and bathrooms, a different color in each. An operable skylight in the master bathroom admits sun or rain from above. Soft jute-sisal flooring helps ensure quiet bedrooms. Sliding glass panels in the northern façade admit breezes above or below. A panel of theatrical scrim conceals kitchen from dining room or catches shadows of people within, depending on light levels. Tall rye grass divides the main-level deck from the pool deck below, suggesting outdoor rooms and adding a sense of natural ground to the weathered deck. In certain lighting conditions the glass reflects the sky, causing the house to appear transparent. At night, the lighting of house and pool allows for warm illumination of the colored cube and tower volumes, while swimming pool lights provide a blue glow outside.

Freeman House

Rhode Island, USA
Estes/Twombly Architects, Inc.

House area: 2600 square feet/242 square meters
Site area: 1.2 acres/0.5 hectare
Materials: exposed fir beams and sheathing, maple floors and cabinets, fieldstone, painted trim and casework, 2x6 wood frame construction with full basement, fir beam roof structure, 1x6 fir sheathing, exterior rigid foam insulation, red cedar shingles for roof and siding, aluminum-clad windows and doors, copper standing seam roof, red cedar board-and-batten siding

The design for this house was driven by three major factors. The waterfront site, with its expansive views to the southeast and sun to the south dictated the placement of major rooms and decks. The living room, dining room/kitchen and common deck are in line along this waterfront façade. The façade itself is composed of large, double-hung windows with wide overhanging eaves to block the summer sun.

The second major design consideration was the requirement for separate but equal sleeping quarters for extended families and the related notion of coming together in the public space. This requirement evolved into the idea of a contemporary and upscale version of an Adirondack camp. The sleeping portion of the structure contains four equally sized bedrooms and serves a large two-story living hall containing the common living, dining, and kitchen areas. The function of the sleeping wing is simple and repetitive, so we made the architecture simple and repetitive. In the Adirondack tradition, the living hall structure is exposed wood and the spaces focus on a massive stone fireplace. The fireplace links the living room and the dining room/kitchen inside and, with the expansive glazing, marks this use on the outside.

A third and more subtle programmatic input was the repeated use of words such as public/private, open/closed, exposed/sheltered. These feelings were expressed to some extent in the bunkhouse/mess hall idea, but we took it one step further in the site and house layout. On the water side, the rooms and the decks are bright and open. On the entry side, the rooms (entry and study) are smaller and more closed. A stone wall and grove of birches note entry into the precinct of the house, and the detailing of the path and the house entry is more intimately scaled than detailing in other places. Off the study and connected to the entry path, is a small terrace with a pergola. This is a sheltered outdoor area in contrast to the expansive waterside deck. On the south, a tapering porch makes this transition from the large, open waterside to the more intimate rear terrace.

Gama Issa House

Alto de Pinheiros, São Paulo, Brazil
Marcio Kogan Architect

House area: 7535 square feet/700 square meters
Site area: 18,300 square feet/1700 square meters

The architect's diary note: São Paulo, 21 January, 2002:

"It is ten o'clock at night. Very hot. I use this moment of rare calm and solitude to design the new house. I look through the window and parked in front of the building is a BMW X5. A young man of about 27 slides out of the car with a stunning blonde fearfully clutching her Prada bag. An almost-black, almost-beggar approaches asking if he can watch the car for R$5. They go into a Japanese restaurant. On the radio, which I will turn off within ten seconds, there is talk of the most recent kidnapping and a prison rebellion. I read my notes of the first meeting with the clients, a couple in advertising. We spoke of an enormous library in the living room with double-height ceilings, enormous windows opening completely to the garden, a 10 x 100-foot (3 x 30-meter) pool, a kitchen with an orange lunch table in the center, two symmetrical marble staircases lit by focused natural light, a precisely detailed work studio, spaces of rare and elegant proportions which always relate to the exterior differently, white textures, a Eero Aarnio ball club chair, minimalism, the 60s, electronic music, Stockhausen, Cage, the latest issue of Visionaire magazine, a recipe for spaghetti al mare and finally, 'My Uncle' by Jacques Tati.

I think of a single enormous volume wrapping everything: a white box. In São Paulo, we don't need to be concerned about environmental coherence, it is total chaos, the most absolute chaos. In this city, the world's ugliest, which overflows energy, vibrant like no other, loved and hated, anything that is projected will be totally integrated into the city. Ah, yes, don't let me forget an enormous wall protecting the house, covered in natural wood (maybe from the last tree of the Amazon), and which, certainly, will be completely covered by graffiti, giving the final touch in perfect harmony with the environment."

Gillespie Residence

Vancouver, British Columbia, Canada
James KM Cheng Architects

House area: 6310 square feet/586 square meters
Site area: 15,500 square feet/1440 square meters
Materials: cast-in-place concrete, aluminum curtain wall glazing, zinc cladding, pre-formed metal paneling, limestone slab tiles, Gypsum board on steel studs, cherry doors and cabinetry. The front entry door is steel and glass quartz crystal.

This private residence for a young family is located on a 15,500-square-foot (1440-square-meter) site in a residential neighborhood close to the University of British Columbia. The plan of the residence is organized around a three-story atrium space with a steel and glass stair structure. At the ground floor, the atrium separates, yet visually connects the formal living and dining spaces from the kitchen and family spaces. At the second floor, the atrium separates the master suite from the children's bedrooms. At the garden level, the atrium separates the exercise area from the office and guest suite.

Large expanses of glass and a skylight over the atrium allow for an interplay of light on the three interconnected levels and afford many views to the exterior ponds and extensively landscaped gardens.

Glazer Residence

Colorado, USA
Appleton & Associates, Inc. – Architects

House area: 16,000 square feet/1486 square meters
Guest houses area: 1600 square feet/149 square meters
Horse barn and caretaker's apartment area: 3550 square feet/311 square meters
Site area: 18 acres/7.3 hectares
Materials: stone masonry retaining walls and base, salvaged barn siding, standing seam metal roof, wood, stone and tile floors, salvaged wood and plaster walls, wood cabinets made from salvaged barn siding, salvaged hand-hewn barn timber posts and beams

The challenge was to create a fun, entertaining vacation retreat for our client's family and friends. The project included an extensive program for a main house, two separate guesthouses, a caretaker's unit and horse barn.

The family compound takes advantage of the magnificent panoramic views, and also has a vernacular presence on the site, reminiscent of an old ranch homestead or mining camp, as if it had grown and been added to over the years. To reduce the impact of the scale of the project and fit it harmoniously on the site, the mass of the large main house was broken into several separate but interconnected gabled, barn-like buildings, with a main entry stair tower that looked like it might have once been a grain silo. Principal material choices were in keeping with the old ranch idea, utilizing standing seam metal roofing, and salvaged barn timbers and siding. The stone base and site walls were designed to appear like ruins, suggesting that the place may have been reconstructed on an older masonry foundation. Salvaged barn wood was also recycled for the interior doors, millwork, trim and cabinetry.

In the interior, the octagonal stair tower was conceived as a fantasy tree house, with the splitlog stair winding its way up around eight interior tree columns made from standing dead Lodgepole pines. The bark was left intact, and dead branches were added to hold hanging lanterns, bird nests, carved animals and other surprises, as well as serving as the stair railing. The finished compound is full of rough-hewn, Wild West romance and nostalgia, but its construction and reliance on salvaged and recycled materials are also environmentally conscientious decisions to which we were committed from the start.

Glencoe Residence

Venice, California, USA
Marmol Radziner and Associates

House area: 2775 square feet/258 square meters
Site area: 5850 square feet/544 square meters
Materials: integral colored plaster, aluminum windows, integral colored concrete floors, oak cabinetry, stainless steel countertops (kitchen), and oak floor (2nd floor)

Marmol Radziner and Associates acted as the architect, contractor and furniture fabricator for the house of the firm's design principal, Ron Radziner and his family. Responding to the surrounding context and lot sizes in Venice, California, the Glencoe Residence is a stepped two-story house. Exterior connections between the ground floor living areas flanked by a garden running the length of the narrow lot maximize the available land.

In keeping with the neighborhood's unique fabric of single-story houses, the house's street-front façade is similar in height and scale. A recessed L-shaped second story minimizes the street impact of the additional floor while creating private and intimate spaces by bisecting the garden into front and rear yards. A master bedroom suite, located in the short leg of the 'L', projects over the linear rear garden. The covered patio below, adjacent to the kitchen, becomes an outdoor dining area, physically expanding the residence's living areas. By utilizing a full-height glazing that extends the length of the house, the design allows the landscape, rather than the physical building itself, to define the edge of the living space. Construction materials further reinforce the seamless transition between exterior and interior environments. The exterior paving, pool finish, and house color integrate shades of gray, sand, and brown with the landscape's native foliage. Earth tones reappear in the interior spaces, evident in the concrete floors and walnut cabinetry.

Inspired by the home's clean design lines, Marmol Radziner and Associates designed and fabricated a collection of interior and exterior furniture. Emphasizing proportion, lack of ornamentation, and an awareness of how materials connect, the house, landscape, and furnishings have become one with the total design.

Gosline Residence

Seattle, Washington, USA
Bohlin Cywinski Jackson

House area: 2100 square feet/195 square meters
Site area: 6000 square feet/557 square meters
Materials: structural steel, plywood panels, polycarbonate glazing, fiber cement siding, exposed wood framing, aluminum-framed windows

This house for a retired couple stretches along a narrow sloping site pitching towards views of an arboretum and the distant Cascade Mountains. The building is positioned to preserve two major trees, a Madrona and a large Deodar cedar.

The owners were particularly open-minded and enthusiastic in encouraging an architecture that reveals the nature and assembly of its basic building materials, including common wood framing, plywood, concrete, steel and glass. The residence was tailored to suit the owners' needs, shaping a home that is both playful and contemplative. The rather open layout includes a master bedroom that overlooks the tall living room, two offices that can be used as guest rooms, and such refinements as a mail-sorting nook shielded by a small sliding barn door. Other elements such as the custom Bubinga front door, which was made in Cameroon, are a result of the owners' interest in African botany.

A spine of steel channels and columns extends the entire length of the house, projecting through its face to support two private decks. Wood studs were often left exposed or revealed behind plywood panels. Screens of cedar framing and polycarbonate glazing stretch along the edges of the carport, extending into the building and, combined with the steel spine, pull one through to the long views. A tracery of horizontal flashing bands and fasteners delicately pattern the house's exterior. The house reveals the particular nature of its site, its owners and the materials with which it is made. The satisfying result is a touching place made with modest means.

Hinge House

Los Angeles, California, USA
Aleks Istanbullu Architects

House area: 7500 square feet/697 square meters
Materials: steel framing, colored stucco, steel beams, steel roof, corrugated metal

An entertainment-industry family of five replaced a neglected house dating from the 1950s, sited on a steep hillside in Los Angeles. The architect designed a three-story home that reflected the use and surroundings of the project by combining a sequence of spaces into the maximum allowable building envelope. The home has three distinct components. The first is a two-story volume that includes children's rooms, a family room, a utility room, home offices, a screening room, and media archives. The second component is a sculpted third-floor master suite that sits amid the foliage of the site's trees, giving it an intimate, tree-house feeling. The third component is a steel-framed, two-story volume below the master suite. This volume is an indoor-outdoor 'hinged' space about which the other two components revolve. A series of situations occurs in this theatrical, yet domestic space—a dining platform, a family room balcony, and a stair wrapped around an interior stone koi pond.

The exterior treatment is colored stucco with punched out windows. Exposed steel beams and roofing add to the industrial-techno look that the client requested. The original, clover-leaf pool is refinished and updated (legend has it that Esther Williams was filmed swimming there). The hybrid interior treatments, surfaces, and volumes throughout the home respond to varied domestic activities and establish the sense of a stage set where daily life is displayed. Furnishings are a mix of both playful and serious pieces, ranging from hand-made art-glass sinks in the master bathroom to a streamlined Italian sofa in the living room.

House on the Hill

Serra da Mantiqueira, Brazil
Carlos Bratke

House area: 2690 square feet/250 square meters
Site area: 2.5 acres/1 hectare
Materials: masonry, wood, concrete, pre-painted steel tiles

The house was built in the hills of Serra da Mantiqueira, about 125 miles (200 kilometers) from São Paulo and almost 6560 feet (2000 meters) high, where the temperature in winter drops to around 20°F (-5°C). The site is complemented by a small river, garden and a beautiful panoramic view.

The project divided the plan into three levels. On the ground floor are the main access, living room and balcony, as well as two bedrooms, a bathroom, pantry, the master bedroom and a kitchen. On the lower floor, taking advantage of the inclination of the land, is the housekeeper's room. On the same floor is the laundry area. Dividing the upper floor, is the guest room, a bathroom and a mezzanine, acting like entertainment room, with views of the ground floor. The structure of the house was planned with exposed brick masonry, inside and outside, alternating wood and concrete. The roof has juxtaposed wood scissors, with slats between, creating a kind of a frieze. Wood beams support the steel tiles of the pre-painted roof.

House Otto

Bergheim, Salzburg, Austria
Peter Ebner + Franziska Ullmann

House area: 3230 square feet/300 square meters
Site area: 10,740 square feet/998 square meters
Materials: brick construction with stucco façade

The beautiful site at the foot of fertile foothills, with a breathtaking view to the Alps, determined the design of this single-family house. The landscape is projected into the house as an image; not as the modern concept of the horizontal, but rather the expressionistic character of the vertical, skyward-oriented landscape.

The single-level structure consists of two parallel parts with an additional short, connecting link. The private areas, such as the children's and adult sleeping rooms, are situated in the northern tract, which has a skylight providing wonderful southern light. The second tract, a somewhat lower elevated stucture, has an open, public character and consists of a large living area with a connected eat-in kitchen. The two tracts, together with the connecting link composed of support functions and a small office, enclose an intimate patio. The stuccoed façade is accented by the introduction of metal particles into the exterior paint. Depending on the quality of light, the façade reacts with changing color; from an orange-red, to a warm terracotta, to a metallic, shining bronze tone. With this, House Otto reflects not only the surrounding beauty of the landscape on its interior, but also on its exterior.

House R 128

Stuttgart, Germany
Werner Sobek

House area: 2691 square feet/250 square meters
Materials: steel, glass

This four-story house was designed as a completely recyclable building that produces no emissions and is self-sufficient in terms of heating energy requirements. The completely glazed building has high-quality, triple-glazed panels featuring a k-value of 0.4. Due to its modular design and assembly by means of mortice-and-tenon joints and bolted joints, it cannot only be assembled and dismantled easily but is also completely recyclable. The electrical energy required for the energy concept and control engineering is produced by solar cells.

Access to the building is via a bridge leading to the top floor. This level accommodates the kitchen and dining areas. The two levels below successively provide living and sleeping areas; the bottom level accommodates the nursery as well as the technical and utility installations. The load-bearing structure of the building consists of a steel frame stiffened by diagonal members and erected on a reinforced concrete raft. The floors consist of heavy-section timber modules. There is no rendering or screeding, eliminating any compound materials that may be difficult or impossible to dispose of. For this reason there are no cables or pipes embedded in the walls. All supply or disposal systems as well as communication lines are housed in metal ducts that run along the façades and are built into the floor and ceiling structures.

The emission-free, zero-heating-energy house utilizes an innovative computer-controlled energy concept that can be checked by telephone or computer. The heat energy radiated into the building by the sun is absorbed by water-filled ceiling panels and transferred to a heat store from which the building is heated in the winter by reversing the heat exchange process. In this mode, the ceiling panels function as heat radiators and additional heating is not needed.

Island House

St. Lawrence River, Ontario, Canada
Shim-Sutcliffe Architects

An agricultural landscape of grassy meadows meeting the St. Lawrence River is the setting for this new residence. A 200-foot-long (61-meter) concrete retaining wall is inserted into the site, parallel to the water's edge. A portion of this wall is occupied by the house and the other section defines an exterior dry garden. A large reflecting pool envelopes the main living space, creating a metaphor of an island. From the road, one reads a low building with a series of terracing green roofs that extend the meadow landscape up and over the house.

The poured-in-place concrete retaining wall was built locally. Douglas fir cladding is used on all elevations of the project, providing a warmth and scale that contrasts with the concrete walls. Two lower horizontal planes are green roofs creating an abstract meadow planted with indigenous clover, rye, and sedum. The biomass acts as extra insulation and saves on cooling and heating costs. Rarely considered as a construction material in architecture, water plays a significant role in this project. By creating a large reflecting pool and combining it with a series of gardens and terraced green roofs, the water defines the site for a new living pavilion. The living pavilion is a tall, luminous room that forms the main living space of the house. The reflecting pool wraps the light-filled pavilion, ensuring that the room also captures reflections on all of its surfaces throughout the day. This living space, the metaphorical island retreat, is wrapped in clear glass below with fiberglass above. Fiberglass was selected because of its more tactile irregular quality and its affinity with crinkly, fibrous rice paper.

This project is informed by the existing landscape, yet creates a new landscape within it. The house is situated on an island, and the pavilion-like living room sits as an island in a large reflecting pool, lined with tall, ornamental grasses. Inside the pool rests another small island, planted with bulrushes and water irises.

Jones Residence

Manhattan Beach, California, USA
SFJones Architects Inc.

House area: 2750 square feet/256 square meters
Site area: 4480 square feet/416 square meters
Materials: Douglas fir windows and cladding, Southern ledgestone cultured stone, Santa Fe copper stone, smooth-troweled exterior plaster, copper standing seam roof, Douglas fir trusses, Southern ledgestone cultured stone wall and fireplace, Daru Daru wood floors, Padauk wood kitchen cabinets, cherry wood cabinets, seafoam granite, glass tile, limestone flooring, ceramic tiles

There were numerous challenges to address in the design of the residence. Among them was the fact that the site is in a fairly dense neighborhood, on a relatively tight lot that cross-sloped 8 feet (2.5 meters) from back to front. The allowable building area for the project was 3100 square feet (290 square meters). In addition, there is a 26-foot (8-meter) height limit and a 2-car garage is required by the city. A tandem car garage was implemented, thus avoiding the façade being taken up by garage doors. A strong axial design was created, to allow spatial interrelationships that have overlapping functions and extend the visual boundaries of the building envelope. Additionally, the use of north-facing clerestory windows, skylights, large amounts of glass, ceiling grazing lights, and 10-foot (3-meter) ceilings, create interior spaces that appear volumetric.

The plan is comprised of four areas: the front living/entertainment room, the family room/kitchen, the guest bedroom/office, and the sleeping rooms. The design takes advantage of the topography by providing four split levels within the two-story house, which allows for the four zones to be segregated and creates a sense of privacy between the functions. The living/entertainment room includes the dining room and more formal living room functions. The family room/kitchen area has a triangular spatial relationship between the kitchen, family room, and exterior spaces. This is the primary living space and allows for a visual connection between all of these functions. The mid-level guest bedroom/office was conceived as an apartment within the house. The main sleeping areas are all located on the upper floor. With their high ceilings and large windows that open up the canopy of the trees, these spaces have an open feel while maintaining a sense of privacy.

Kangaloon House

New South Wales, Australia
Peter Stronach, Allen Jack + Cottier

House area: 2476 square feet/230 square meters
Site area: 100 acres/40.5 hectares
Materials: concrete block, galvanized iron

The house, in the Southern Highlands of New South Wales, was designed by Peter Stronach, the Managing Director of Allen Jack + Cottier. Tim Allison, one of Sydney's finest interior designers, designed the interiors in collaboration with Peter Stronach.

The house is positioned to catch the northern sun and to enjoy the breathtaking views to the east. Sitting high among the hills, the house commands extensive views over a rolling landscape that falls away to the east and southeast. Stronach and Allison's major design concept was to create a house that was strongly related to a traditional farmhouse. Given the cold climate, the designers sought to develop maximum energy efficiency through careful use of materials, construction techniques, and appropriate heating, ventilation and lighting systems. It is a house that puts a contemporary twist on the conventional farm or country house. It is built in the form of a barn-like pavilion. The rooms are designed in an almost 19th-century scale and proportion. Each living area can be closed off to retain heat. Upstairs the master and guest bedrooms are separated by the void above the kitchen, providing a sense of space and privacy.

The house uses energy-saving techniques to keep warm in winter and cool in summer. During cold periods, unused parts of the house can be readily closed off, keeping the heat in. All ground-floor rooms enjoy large windows to maximise the winter sun, and the windows are double-glazed to minimize heat loss, including an all-glass verandah room. Small openings have been used in all first-floor rooms to control heat loss at night and heat gain on summer days.

Peter's most innovative design feature was to use materials in the walls that would insulate the house to keep the heat out in summer and contain it in winter. There is no need for air conditioning, as the rooms on both floors have been designed to allow cross-ventilation, allowing fresh air to flow throughout the house. To achieve optimum thermal performance, the ground floor external walls were made of reverse masonry veneer, consisting of high efficiency 'Astrofoil' insulation between an inner skin of concrete blockwork covered with MiniOrb corrugated steel sheeting fixed to timber studwork. Throughout the ground floor, polished concrete has been used for floors, exposed honed-face concrete blockwork for walls, and hoop pine-veneered plywood on ceilings.

Kilburn Residence

Western Australia, Australia
Iredale Pedersen Hook Architects

House area: 4036 square feet/375 square meters
Site area: 5640 square feet/524 square meters
Materials: rendered brick paint finish, industrial metallic paint to study render (walls); concrete slab on ground with cross-cut travertine stone to living, dining and kitchen (floors); BHP Gull Grey Colorbond (roof); powder-coated aluminum and clear anodized aluminum (exterior doors); paint finish hollowcore doors in folded steel frame (interior doors)

The brief from the client included the following requirements: the design must maximize the amount of accommodation at ground level, the upper level being mainly for guests; all major rooms at ground level must have a northern aspect with plenty of natural light in winter but stop the direct summer sun (except the main bedroom); and all major rooms should look directly onto courtyards.

Instead of the more traditional back and front gardens, courtyards were developed as a series of intimate, but linked, spaces. The largest relates to the main living space and includes a long strip of falling water and pond. The building extends to protect this courtyard from the rain-bearing northwest and west winds, and to provide protection from the strong southwest winds, while still maintaining the cooling effects of the southwest winds by cross-ventilation through the house. This courtyard has year-round use with a built-in, retractable awning providing shade from the sun in summer and from the rain in winter. The second courtyard and the study relate to the street while providing a degree of privacy to the main courtyard. The most intimate courtyard is to the south.

The entry is covered by a glazed canopy that protects one from the elements while maintaining an open feel. The stair connection between the two levels is considered to be a major event, simultaneously reinforcing its role as connection and separation of two different worlds. This is clad in translucent glass and from the outside will shine at night like a giant lantern or beacon. The upper-level roof shape expands to the source of light and garden view, creating these as a focal point for the rooms within (all upper bedrooms have raked ceilings).

Kimber House

Perth, Western Australia, Australia
Patroni Architects

The foremost item of the brief was the tennis court and this became the context for the project as the game of tennis and its device became an analogy for the program—a modern family with demands for fluctuating numbers and a variety of lifestyles. The spaces both within and outside the house flow like an exploded tennis court; the tramline-like spine wall allows a variety of family configurations to optimally enjoy the place at one time.

All north-facing glass is shaded by cantilevered shade structures that permit winter sun and exclude summer sun. There are very few openings to the east or west. The boundary between inside and outside has been deliberately blurred. The shifting levels allow one space to 'float' while another space seems to be firmly earthed; the living areas extend beyond the pivoting timber doors without changing level or material, and then begin to terrace down past the swimming pool, via a lily pond that reveals itself as the roof of the tennis court pavilion. The water garden is let in using long, low windows at floor level, excluding the view of an adjoining property while allowing the reflected light of the moving water to animate the interior of the apartment side of the house, emphasizing its 'floating' quality. By day, the house is flooded with natural light; at night lighting is used both inside and out to emphasize the integration between the two.

The architectural language of the project is different from its neighbors, some of which were designed 80–90 years ago, while some contemporary houses are imitations of, or references to past styles. It was our intention that the project be proudly of its time, helping to log architectural development from the past, present and future. The local authority did not share this position and the project did not receive planning consent for 12 months, and then only via ministerial appeal. Nevertheless, the project is in scale with its neighbors and an overall integration with the neighborhood and its character has been achieved, while also making a vibrant contribution to the streetscape.

Leesa and Sam's House

Christmas Lake, Excelsior, Minnesota, USA
Charles R. Stinson Architects

House area: 3200 square feet/297 square meters
Site area: 1 acre/0.4 hectare
Materials: stucco, green windows, green roof, bamboo floors, maple and Corian cabinets

Leesa Nahki-Brown, a mother with a preteen son, had a simple wish: 'I wanted a home that we could really live in and where Sam would feel good bringing his friends.' She also specified a small office space, a laundry next to the bedrooms, a built-in buffet, kitchen island, and unique fireplace. The two-bedroom lakeside house is a De Stijl-like composition of sophisticated simplicity, Modrianesque planes of primary colors juxtaposed with white, and open space filled with light. Two-story windows in a square arch allow views straight through the white-stucco house to the lake, with overhangs positioned to allow in light during the winter and block hot sun in the summer.

'Leesa asked us to design the interiors and she wanted color,' Stinson says, 'so we did an abstraction of primary colors and made a Modrian composition out of them'. One early winter morning during construction, he saw the main level aglow with light from the rising sun reflected off the lake. 'When sun came into the great room, the space was transformed into a golden temple,' he recalls, 'so we built on this experience using bamboo floors and painting the ceiling a deep yellow to extend that golden moment.' Color is also found on the main level in the red-painted forms of the glass-block-framed fireplace. On the other end of the first floor are the dining room and kitchen, separated by a built-in floating buffet with a glass plane intersected by vertical square arch shelving that echoes the fireplace composition across the room.

The square arch theme is also found in the white Corian that wraps the maple cabinets and the built-in flower vase holder atop the curved-maple butcher block and black-granite island. A small study is located behind the kitchen. The entire first floor opens onto a patio overlooking the lawn extending to the lake. The second level includes two bedrooms separated by a daylit gallery. Sam's small suite contains a walk-in closet and bath. Leesa's suite includes a fireplace framed with green-painted forms and white walls. Off their bedrooms, mother and son share a large balcony that overlooks the lake.

Lexton MacCarthy Residence

Silver Lake, California, USA
Lorcan O'Herlihy Architects

House area: 2000 square feet/186 square meters

Isolating the hillside house as a building type is very important for architectural discourse. Sloping sites offered California modernists, Wright, Schindler, Neutra, Lautner, and others, the opportunity to invent new forms, transforming the house. Continuing in this tradition, this site offered wonderful west-facing views of Los Angeles and suggested a formal strategy of an abstract geometrical form conceived as a play of positive and negative volumes.

The house sits on a steeply sloping lot. The siting of the house, carport and stair was conceived as a 'straight dislocation'. The carport breaks away from the house with its path traced by a connecting stairway. Given the limited square footage of the house, the primary floor is conceived as a free plan, which allows for programmatic flexibility. The second story houses the master bedroom suite. The section of the second floor traces an area on the first floor that houses the kitchen, stair, bathroom and closet. The building fenestration on the west wall at the living room is receding and the fenestration at the core of the house reinforces the vertical line through the glu-laminated columns. The house is wrapped in 1x6 pine horizontal siding that floats away from the structure with 2x2-inch vertical spacers. The second floor siding is stained blue.

The internal plan and distribution of program is suggested in the treatment of the exterior skin. The idea of the house is to establish a horizontal layer on the primary floor and vertical volume on the second floor. A new vocabulary for wood structures was proposed. The formal simplicity allows for a greater focus on materials, proportions, and details. A research component of the project brought us to identify Frank Lloyd Wright's Usonian houses as a point of departure. Opposing the idea that a building should reveal its construction at first glance, this solution blurs that criterion and allows the skin to wrap structure, glass, concrete or plywood.

Lovall Valley Residence

Napa County, California, USA
Cass Calder Smith Architecture

House area: 2500 square feet/232 square meters
Site area: 10 acres/4 hectares

Located in Napa County, this residence is a second home for a writer, a painter and their two young children. The couple had a vision for a country retreat that would merge with the outdoors, contrasting with their own urban residence. They were interested in earthen walls and other sustainable elements—sheet-rocked surfaces were to be avoided. A place expressive of 'rural simplicity' became the collaborative goal.

A two-building scheme, linked by a covered breezeway and nestled into a 100-year-old grove of oaks, forms the general plan for the home. The breezeway acts as a point of organization and contemplation, linking the entry path to the pool and golden fields beyond. East and west from the breezeway are the two buildings—one for living, one for sleeping. The intent is to add additional small structures over time, continuing the vernacular of multiple buildings with a variety of type, use, and age. The buildings take maximum advantage of their southern orientation and embrace a swimming pool on its own level, 18 inches (0.5 meters) below. The north and west sides of the buildings, situated close to the oaks, experience both a connection to the trees and a contrast in light quality.

Sixteen-inch-thick (0.4-meter) shot-earth walls comprise the east–west portion of the living building, while the north–south walls are wood, sided inside and out with cedar. The living room, with large double doors at each end, becomes a similar space to the breezeway. The roof framing is all exposed, a combination of reclaimed old-growth cedar and painted structural steel. Ground-level floors are integral color concrete with hydronic radiant heating.

M House

La Escondida Beach, Cañete, Peru
Barclay & Crousse Architecture, Paris

The project emerged from a process of reflection on certain factors that we considered essential: the climatic conditions of the Peruvian coast, the geographical characteristics of the coast in which the dwelling was to be located, and the client's needs.

The Peruvian desert is one of the most arid ones in the world, with temperatures ranging from 55°F minimum in winter to 90°F maximum in summer (13°C–30°C), with very little variation between day and night. These characteristics determined two basic strategies. The first one is the ambiguity between exterior and interior spaces within an enclosed space that clearly separates private and public domains, usually seen in local popular houses. The second one is the use of sand and red colors that prevent the building from visually 'aging' as it gathers layers of desert dust.

The house is conceived as a plain rectangular volume, excavated by narrow, open spaces conceived as cracks in hardened sand, protected from wind and sun, where circulation develops following the natural topography. These open spaces merge with closed ones through a double-height loggia, framing the sea and the island in front of it. The house is divided into three distinct volumes. The first is composed of the garage and the entrance. The children's bedrooms and the guestroom occupy the central volume. The parents' bedroom is located above the kitchen/dining/living room space constituting the third volume. The living/dining room configures the main space of the house and its double-height space is the link between the ocean and the inner open spaces. From this space, the house is revealed in all of its height, width and length, giving the dweller a feeling of spaciousness in a quite small house.

Maison Katz–Reniers

Rue des Pêcheurs, Brussels, Belgium
Victor Lévy, Architect

This house faced two design problems: first, it was the last one to be built in a street where neighbors enjoyed the fact that the lot was left empty; second, the house needed deep foundations as the lot was made of infill soil at the location of a former pond.

The decision to use wood for both the structure and its exterior cladding reduced the weight of the building by about 70 percent. In addition, it responded to some anxiety in the neighborhood: a wooden house was likely to appear lighter and less imposing than a brick and concrete one. The clients were also attracted by the concept of a lightweight, wide-open house that evokes the hut in the woods. The architect maximized the advantages of a mode of construction that permits thin supports and, well-crafted, allows for suggestive effects with materials.

The hall distributes both levels of the house, which are prolonged by wide terraces on the garden side. The street façade, only glazed at the second-floor with tall windows, appears as a long palisade, carefully mounted. At ground level, the circulation spaces, lined with continuous glass walls and parallel terraces, bring spatial fluidity and create an interesting indoor-outdoor relationship that emphasizes the quiet horizontality. The interior walls, stuccoed and painted white, erase the presence of the wood, while increasing the sense of lightness and transparency with the outside. The two-level hallway and the upstairs bedrooms seem to grow taller, a lifting volumetric impression that is reinforced by the semi-cylindrical roof. The second-floor terrace, paved like the first-floor one and connected to it with numerous supports, evokes the deck of a ship. This suggestion—that contrasts with the general sense of space—is furthered by the use of porthole windows in the doors, a reference to naval construction and mobile architecture. Overall, this volumetric diversity, at times horizontal, at times vertical, gives a strong architectural identity to the interior of the house.

Malibu Residence

Malibu, California, USA
Shubin + Donaldson Architects

House area: 2900 square feet/269 square meters
Materials: cement pavers, river rock, frosted glass, wenge wood, limestone

This beach-side modern house is perched along Malibu's Pacific Coast Highway, and features access to the beach at the rear. A transitional interior entry courtyard introduces the primary design element of the home—a seamless union between interior and exterior spaces, with crisp linear architecture, and visual access throughout. From the entry courtyard, an original space accented by a grid of windowpanes houses the dining room. The grid is echoed by the geometric pattern of the cabinets and shelves that lead into the minimal kitchen. True to the open plan, the kitchen overlooks the main living space.

The ground-floor living room and adjacent sitting room offer respite from the sunlit terraces beyond, with cooling white and dark wood tones in the furniture and materials. Double-paned windows, which open onto the first-level terrace, permit unrestricted views onto the ocean while buffering sound from the highway.

The upstairs rooms continue the overall theme of air, light, and water with repeating materials and colors. The master suite faces onto a second large terrace with pocket-glass doors that fold away, converting the stepped upper terrace into a sleeping porch. Openness and transformation are themes throughout and are most expressive in the master bath. Cool, ocean-blue frosted glass lines the walls and windows. Three layers of floor-to-ceiling glass form a translucent door that closes the space off from the bedroom, or opens it up to the master suite, porch, and Pacific Ocean beyond. Dark wenge wood—used throughout the house as an accent—encases the tub, vanity, and spacious closets. Double mirrors are placed on poles in front of the frosted glass, rather than set into a wall.

Mankins–Camp Residence

San Francisco, California, USA
Herbert Lewis Kruse Blunck Architecture

House area: 2800 square feet/260 square meters
Materials: masonry (to match existing), integrally colored plaster, English slate, beech, cherry casework/paneling

This residence in San Francisco is home for a self-declared anal-retentive management consultant and his pathologist partner. After a two-year search for the perfect home, this couple came across a home designed by noted Frank Lloyd Wright associate Aaron Greene. The house was in some disrepair, having been on the market for nearly six months and, while the home's design pedigree provided the structure with 'good bones' and the site afforded a spectacular view, it had fallen victim to four decades of ill-fated remodeling efforts. The resulting home had no clear organization and a tired material palette with only glimpses of the original character remaining. The couple directed the architect, the twin brother of the management consultant (also anal-retentive) to research the home and substantially remodel it to fit their needs.

In investigating the home, an underlying order was discovered. The home originally employed a strategy which placed the building's 'serving' spaces, largely solid and unfenestrated, toward the front, street side of the home, reserving the back of the home for the 'served' spaces and providing them with full access to the panoramic view. In addition, the plan strictly adhered to a 4-foot (1.2-meter) planning module. The architect extended and clarified the underlying parti in the remodeling. In addition, the stair was reoriented and placed to the side of the entry hall. This modification created a central hall at the lower level and simplified the circulation on both levels. Fundamentally, the plan was reduced to a series of contiguous spaces that flow together, fitting the lifestyle of the homeowners. The stunning view, previously under-utilized, now animates nearly every space in the home.

Mason House

Sydney, New South Wales, Australia
Chenchow Little Architects

House area: 2583 square feet/240 square meters
Site area: 53,820 square feet/5000 square meters
Materials: rendered brickwork, plasterboard, zincalume coated steel, forbo marmoleum, stone tile

The large rectangular site is densely planted with trees, and a row of mature cypress pines forms a hedge along the eastern boundary adjacent to the existing holiday residence. The Mediterranean-style residence was built around the 1930s and features stucco walls, arched arcades and timber shutters. The interior is dark and introverted, being almost completely shut off from the established garden.

The existing dwelling comprised three bedrooms, a bathroom, living areas and a small kitchen. The kitchen was totally separate from the remainder of the dwelling. The clients wished to add a new eat-in kitchen, bathroom and master bedroom to enable the house to accommodate visiting family members. The addition was also required to open the house to the garden. The final addition responds to the form and style of the existing dwelling.

The addition is made up of four main components; massive walls, a lightweight roof, a raised platform and a bridge. The new massive walls replicate the width of the existing colonnade on the northern façade. The wall cavities conceal the bathroom vanity, the kitchen cabinetry and building services. The new roof has been designed to follow the pitch of the existing terracotta roof. Steelwork has been used to give the roof the thinnest profile possible and the minimum number of supports, resulting in a roof that appears to hover above the new eat-in kitchen. The kitchen opens onto a north-facing terrace with views to the garden and tennis court. The addition is separated from the existing dwelling by the bridge, which floats above the ground. The bridge marks the junction between the old and new parts of the dwelling and occurs on axis with a small courtyard, which separates the kitchen from the master bedroom.

Matchbox House

North Fork, Long Island, New York, USA
Gluckman Mayner Architects

House area: 3600 square feet/335 square meters
Materials: wood frame, wood composition joists, integral composite plywood, poured-in-place concrete, Minerit concrete panels, cedar siding, mahogany doors and windows, maple flooring, maple plywood millwork for cabinets, shelving and ceiling, gypsum wall board, black granite for kitchen floor, Carrara marble for kitchen countertops and backsplash, glazed ceramic tile and ceramic tile mosaics for bathroom walls and floors

The Matchbox House is a weekend beach house, designed to maximize the picturesque landscape near the water's edge. The interior is fully integrated with the outdoors—elevated living spaces and the kitchen area on the second floor lead out onto open decks, taking advantage of the sea breeze to cool and circulate throughout the house in the summer months. Bedrooms and bathrooms are stacked on the second and third floors; the master bedroom on the top floor continues outward onto a private rooftop deck. The deck leads upward toward the horizon of the sky, offering a panoramic view yet providing exclusive privacy.

Montecito Hillside Residence

Montecito, California, USA
Ronald Frink Architects, Inc.

House area: 4600 square feet/427 square meters
Guest house area: 800 square feet/74 square meters
Site area: 1.2 acres/0.5 hectares
Materials: exterior plaster, square cut, cleft finished, Arizona Flagstone (terraces); natural maple hardwood, honed squares of Jerusalem limestone (floors); custom casework in natural maple (kitchen, family room and master suite); custom natural maple windows with dual glazing; brushed stainless steel hardware; steel footbridge; polished Carioca Gold granite (kitchen countertops, family room, living/dining room fireplaces); spiral staircase with custom plaster surround, solid maple tread, brushed stainless steel handrails (guesthouse); custom solid maple plank stair users and treads (main house)

The contemporary residence and guest house are situated in the gentle-sloping foothills of Montecito, California, with panoramic views of Santa Barbara Harbor, the Pacific Ocean and surrounding mountains. The irregular-shaped site has substantial landscape frontage at the roadway, affording the residence tremendous privacy. A serpentine driveway and garden wall lead from the street entry gate to the motor court at the front of the house. The entry garden court leads to the main house entry gallery and step-down living room with panoramic coastal views. The main house is a graceful two-story contemporary villa with extensive terraces and lawn areas for easy indoor and outdoor living. A three-sided custom cantilevered fireplace serves both the living and dining rooms. The open kitchen and family room anchor the north end of the gallery and the guest room and upper master suite anchor the south end of the gallery adjacent to the pool and spa terrace. All curves for the terraces, infinity pool, stone retaining walls and the guest house bay window originate from the intersection of the cross axes, adding to the spatial harmony of the design.

Across a wooded dry creek, a 50-foot (15-meter) footbridge links the infinity pool/spa terrace at the main house to the guesthouse, conceived as a playful and tranquil retreat from the main house. The guesthouse is situated in an acacia grove on a dry creek bed toward the rear of the property, offering complete privacy in a square two-story volume with a sleeping loft in the upper quarter of the plan. Large two-story windows and a curved bay window provide wonderful daylight and filtered views through the trees with glimpses of the ocean horizon. A new dry creek bed was designed under the footbridge to help with on-site storm drainage and to reinforce the natural setting of the native creek bed. Some 8–10 feet (3 meters) above grade, a large deck extends from the main floor of the guesthouse, extending the living space on this level. The gallery axis of the main house leads from the north garden to the pool/spa terrace and across the footbridge to the lower deck of the guesthouse. The footbridge is supported on concrete piers at each end, and is threaded through the canopy of the oak trees.

Montecito Residence

Montecito, California, USA
Shubin + Donaldson Architects

House area: 3800 square feet/353 square meters
Materials: shed roof, steel trusses, metal decking, plaster, glass, maple wood

Situated in Montecito, California, an upscale hillside community adjacent to Santa Barbara, this residence is one of few contemporary designs in the area. The clients, a retired couple, desired a restrained and economical building in which to enjoy their substantial art collection, and the dynamic site that features mountain and ocean views. The architects' goal was to design a contemporary, urban, loft-like home in a very traditional neighborhood. The three-bedroom residence is distinctly organized with one main axis or circulation/gallery that runs along the whole structure. The center of the building features the public areas of living, dining, and

kitchen, with circulation walls functioning as the desired gallery space for artwork. The open plan emphasizes space usage and contemporary living. A sculptural glass-and-steel fireplace separates the living area from the dining room. The far north-end block serves as the master bedroom and bath. The two-bedroom guest quarters are at the opposite end, adjacent to a three-car garage.

A modern and inviting environment was achieved by layering the mix of building and finish materials, by maintaining a constant visual connection with the outdoors, and by flooding the spaces with light, with the aid of ten skylights throughout. The dwelling is covered by a shed roof built with steel trusses and metal decking. This structure is revealed at the dramatic entry and along the main axis circulation/gallery to express its place within the overall design vocabulary. The walls of the house are primarily plaster and glass. Maple flooring and cabinetry add warmth and intimacy to the public areas, while subtle hues of tinted plaster soften the composition of intersecting planes on the interior and exterior.

Mountain Tree House

Dillard, Georgia, USA
Mack Scogin Merrill Elam Architects

House area: 1000 square feet/93 square meters
Open deck area: 1000 square feet/93 square meters
Materials: cast-in-place concrete, steel, and wood framing (structure)

The Mountain House was built five years prior. It is an inside-outside place. Half screened porch and outdoor courtyards; half inside house and glass walls. Set for gardening and reading, it is a weekend retreat into the vertical poplar trunks among the foothills of the Appalachian Mountains. But now the family has grown with grandchildren and friends, and a little more space is needed for things like tractors and dogs. The new project is a concrete garage, a steel bedroom and a bamboo deck. It too is an inside-outside thing, but also an up-down and heavy-light thing.

The garage is for working and gardening, the storage of tools and the occasional car. It is walled by unfinished concrete, with plain doors and long windows. The bedroom above is cantilevered over the work-yard, as open with glass walls as the garage is closed below. The little bathroom is solid, clad in steel. The walls swing open for outdoor showers and spring cleaning. The bamboo starts with planters on the ground and grows up through a narrow slot in the deck above. The space is for sitting and viewing, in and among the fast-growing canes. The structure is wood and steel framing atop reinforced concrete walls. Deck surface and interior flooring is black slate. The ramp and handrails are self-weathering steel. Panels of the same steel, lap-jointed and welded, clad the upper room. Glass walls are either clear tempered or translucent laminated.

New House

Paraparaumu, Kapiti Coast, New Zealand
Bevin + Slessor Architects Ltd

House area: 2100 square feet/195 square meters
Site area: 5 acres/2 hectares
Materials: clear-finished plywood ceilings, painted walls, polished concrete floors, timber floors, exposed double macrocarpa rafters

The existing home on the site, a 1950's imported prefabricated cottage, had enjoyed the views across the west-facing, 5-acre (2-hectare) farmlet to Kapiti Island. The family of four had outgrown this cottage but the siting was ideal for a new house. The cottage was relocated lower down on the site and a new dwelling designed to engage the views and sun, utilizing economic low-maintenance materials and a simple architectural form. While the brief called for five bedrooms and a separate living space, the siting, budget and ground conditions determined a lightweight, single-story dwelling. The siting was on the crest of a terrace, close to a mature stand of New Zealand bush, to which the house also needed to relate and engage. Siting the house along the east–west axis faced the westward views out to Kapiti Island and the afternoon sun. The effects of the prevailing westerly winds and traffic noise from State Highway 1 are offset by the ability to open the house along the north–south axis. Ventilation on the western side is provided largely through timber louvers.

The house was conceived as two gabled pavilions. The 'sleeping' pavilion and the 'living' pavilion. To define the two forms, each pavilion was given a different material treatment. The longer 'sleeping' pavilion was clad in dark corrugated colorsteel, while the forward more open and light 'living' pavilion was clad in a combination of plywood, gapped cedar battens over painted cement boarding, and corrugated zincalume. The strong Kapiti Coast sunlight is filtered and reflected through timber screens and louvers. The adjustable timber louvers also provide cross-ventilation through the rooms while the windows remain as large glazed openings, free of window mechanisms facing west. The dining area was located at the core of the living pavilion, allowing for circulation between the formal living and informal kitchen and sitting areas and also opening out to the west. The circulation through the central hallway between the two pavilions offers a view through the length of the building.

This house received a NZIA-Resene Award in 2002 for, among other things, its 'refreshing departure from flat roof Modernism.'

Ortega Ridge Residence

Summerland, California, USA
B3 Architects, a Berkus Design Studio

House area: 5765 square feet/535 square meters
Site area: 1.8 acres/0.75 hectare
Materials: roofing: standing seam copper, built up roofing, waterproof traffic topping; cladding: exterior cement plaster, integral color acrylic finish, copper fascias; window systems: aluminum sash and doors, anodized finish, tinted glass; trellis and canopies: painted steel, sandblasted glass; paving: acid wash, integral color concrete driveways, flagstone at terraces, pool deck; limestone flooring; limestone and copper fireplace; walls and ceilings: drywall, stained birch ceiling in morning room

The creation of a structure on this highly visible hilltop site presented a challenge that resulted in the sculpting of a highly articulated silhouette that accommodates axial living functions while capturing a 360-degree view. Santa Barbara County's ridge-top ordinances also mandated a low-scale form. This structure mitigates the intense sun and wind patterns by orientation and courtyard footprint, while taking advantage of its south solar orientation. The constructed form capitalizes on its hilltop vistas by functioning as a series of pavilions oriented to distant views. Glass walls lend transparency to the home, allowing patterns of landscape and light to be enjoyed within the structure. Limestone-clad sentinels capped with glass clerestories illuminate the interior passageways.

The entry courtyard provides an alternative outdoor living space, protected from the wind. A material palette of limestone, steel, copper, plaster and glass articulates the forms that crown the hill. The copper-clad roof shapes reference the curved forms of surrounding mountains and echo the character of leaves falling in the wind. The sentinels reference the strength of trees and lighthouses found on the coastal plain. A series of pools bisect the interior living space and disappear with an infinity edge toward the ocean. In keeping with the natural arid climate, the landscape vegetation is drought-resistant.

Palm Desert Residence

California, USA
B3 Architects, a Berkus Design Studio

House area: 5000 square feet/465 square meters
Materials: roofing: built up roofing; cladding: exterior cement plaster, painted finish, integral color concrete; window systems: aluminum clad wood sash and doors, Kynar finish, tinted glass; canopies: painted steel; exposed steel columns, painted finish; flooring: integral color concrete with exposed glass aggregate decorative pattern, tile, carpet; glass and ceramic tile; drywall, painted finish walls and ceilings

Bisected by a gently curving arc that references the main street of a village, this desert dwelling comprises a series of sculpted forms paying homage to its environment and the hills beyond. This structure departs from traditional design through the use of highly sculpted form. Rooms within the dwelling are sculpted in different geometric shapes, creating unique destinations with view configurations focusing on the surrounding desert landscape. A series of multi-colored sentinels surrounded by desert gardens denote a path leading to the front of the home. Similar to sculpture, the structure visually and physically entices movement through and about its forms.

The curved hall is the main circulation element leading to passive and active areas within. Glazed portals at each end of the hallway lead to exterior gardens. An elevated roof terrace over the sitting room views the city lights to the east. A centrally located pool and spa create a separation between the living and sleeping functions off the central ribbon axis with views of the landscaped fairways intersecting at the rear of the home. The color palette utilizes subtle desert tones, enabling this otherwise bold configuration of shapes to be in harmony with the desert community.

Palo Alto House

Palo Alto, California, USA
Swatt Architects

House area: 6075 square feet/632 square meters
Site area: 15,250 square feet/1416 square meters
Materials: steel and wood frame over concrete pier and grade beam foundation, integral color stucco, cast-in-place concrete, redwood siding, Minnesota limestone panels, clear glass in clear anodized aluminum frames, Jerusalem limestone, maple hardwood and ceramic tile flooring, painted gypsum board walls, redwood soffits, painted steel columns, precast concrete and brushed stainless steel fireplace

The owners brought to this project a passion for architecture, a wealth of ideas and a desire to create an artistic family home with unique materials and details. The result is a lively composition of dynamic spaces, rich materials and intricate detailing.

The design started with the concept of dividing the building program into two major wings: a 'public' and adult wing, and a guest and children's wing. A dramatic double-height central entrance gallery links the two wings and contains the principal horizontal and vertical circulation for the house. This gallery juxtaposes a cast-in-place concrete wall on the street side with a two-story glass curtain wall on the garden side. The curtain wall extends the interior spaces into the garden and provides visual links between the separate wings of the house.

A steel-framed stair, clad in maple, floats between the walls of the gallery, folding around a glass wall suspended from a stainless steel cable support system.

A major theme of the house is light. By day, natural light enters the house from a number of dramatic sources. The garden side curtain wall bathes the public spaces of the house with light, a skylight over the glass bridge of the library sends a shaft of light into the living room below, and two large oculus skylights highlight the concrete wall of the gallery. At night, soft light from the interior makes the house glow like a lantern in the garden. Vibrantly painted walls, unique light fixtures, modern furniture and an extensive collection of contemporary art complement the complex architectural composition.

Park Presidio Residence

San Francisco, California, USA
Kuth Ranieri

House area: 6500 square feet/418 square meters
Site area: 3000 square feet/279 square meters
Materials: clear anodized aluminum storefront, swage locked aluminum bar grating, Frit (Etchmate) glass, rubber-clad wall, Comberbrune limestone (French), clear and bleached quarter-sawn maple, blackened steel, orbital sanded plexiglass, epoxy terrazzo gallery flooring

This residence is sited in a dense urban residential area adjacent to San Francisco's Park Presidio. The house captures sweeping views of the Park's open space, with distant views to the Golden Gate Bridge and the Pacific Ocean. The program is stacked on four levels, intertwining formal and informal vertical circulation with domestic programming and gallery exhibition. A 75-foot-long (23-meter) gallery links the public zones of the ground floor with the main vertical stair core, entry and garden. The gallery is a more institutional space, with terrazzo floors, and commercial rubber stair treads and lighting systems. This contrasts with the more inviting rooms that flank the gallery accommodating living, dining, and family kitchen.

The construction of the façade is of integral color smooth-troweled plaster, punctuated by an aluminum storefront glazing system. We avoided the figure of the postage stamp garden—the 'front yard sign'—by excavating the entire width of the lot, bifurcating the sloped site into a bridge and a ramp. The typical condition of garage door and front door, side by side, brought forth a strategy of vehicular ramp down to the garage and metal entry bridge to the front door. The entry bridge continues the material, dimension and language of the sidewalk, pulling it deep into the interior to define the public realm and gallery.

The program called for a fully self-sufficient energy system. In response, the roof surface is covered with of a field of crystalline silicon photovoltaic modules with a 150-square-foot (14-square-meter) photovoltaic skylight of laminated glass and amorphous cellular technology enclosing the main stair. It is one of this product's first applications in the United States. In the stairwell, beneath the skylight, filtered sunlight registers the pattern of its purpose, illuminating the translucent handrails and the surfaces of adjoining rooms and foyer below.

Private Residence

Wyoming, USA
Dubbe~Moulder Architects

Materials: standard wood frame construction accented with log columns and beams, wood shingles, wood plank and chink siding, ledge-laid stone and brick veneers; walnut doors and cabinetry, quarter-sawn white oak trim and floors, connecting bridge made of aged Douglas fir.

"The erection of structures devoid of beauty is mere building, a trade and not an art. Edifices in which strength and stability alone are sought, and in designing which only utilitarian considerations have been followed are properly works of engineering. Only when the idea of beauty is added to that of use does a structure take its place among works of Architecture."
A.D.F. Hamlin

The beauty of this residence results from the careful planning of a unique composition of landscape, building and site that respects the neighbors and complements the natural surroundings. Maintaining and expanding on the inherent beauty of the physical site was a paramount design consideration, as was providing spectacular views of distant mountain ranges or closer scenes of wildlife in a nearby watercourse. Water was a primary design feature and was incorporated throughout the site by way of recirculating ponds designed to sustain cutthroat trout throughout the year. The ponds are connected by a flowing, babbling brook that is brought through the house by a connecting bridge that links private parts of the house to public ones.

The design of the main house is a careful adaptation of the American Shingle style, with references to the great mountain lodges of the Northwestern United States. A variety of terraces provide outdoor entertaining space or a peaceful, natural setting to curl up with a book. The guesthouse was designed with garage space below and living space above with large balconies to make the most of panoramic vistas. The landscape design salvaged existing cottonwood trees and added aspen and Colorado blue spruce, carefully placed in order to block views to neighboring properties. The final touch was the addition of natural grasses and wildflower sod to balance the small patches of manicured lawn.

Rancho Dos Vidas

Frio County, Texas, USA
Michael G. Imber, Architect

House area: 4600 square feet/427 square meters
Materials: Colorado river sand colored plaster, Spanish barrel clay tile roof, Oklahoma sugarloaf flagstone paving, stained concrete, Texas leuders cut-stone surround at main entry, mesquite entry doors, all other windows and doors custom mahogany, natural sand plaster interior, antique long-leaf pine wood beams at ceiling, decorative talavera tile, hand-wrought-iron hardware, custom-made copper lighting fixtures, custom leaded glass windows, mahogany cabinets

Located in the scrub country between San Antonio and Laredo, Rancho Dos Vidas draws its forms, geometry, and details from the Spanish Colonial archetypes of south Texas and northern Mexico. The primary force behind the program and plan is the 'event of the hunt,' allowing the elements and their organization to be informed by the process of hunting in Texas while offering a variety of experiential spaces. The main court features a courtyard fountain, and offers comfort through the intimate scale of the gathering space for both arrival and departure while providing a connection to the supporting service court through a grand arch. The pavilion is linked to the lodge though the mud and gunrooms.

A door of mesquite opens to the lofty, beamed entry hall and into the great room. Transecting the hall, a plaster-vaulted gallery provides the organizational cross-axis for the house. Anchored by the master bedroom wing at one end and by the guesthouse tower at the other, the gallery also serves as a main circulation spine for the second bedroom, great room, powder room, and dining room. Running parallel to the gallery, the veranda is divided into two parts by the great room. The private east veranda serves the family's quarters, while the more public west veranda serves to shade the dining room and offers outdoor dining with spectacular views.

The kitchen expands into the veranda by arches in-filled with large ornamental windows that open onto a protected kitchen courtyard, which connects to the gunroom, mudroom, and service court. The kitchen courtyard is the center of the public aspects of the lodge: the kitchen, service wing, and guest quarters tower all focus around a splashing fountain and are shaded by a bougainvillea-covered loggia. Through the loggia, a raised pool terrace spreads to overlook the fire pit, an outpost to the wilderness and favorite evening gathering spot.

Ranger Point House

Seatoun, Wellington, New Zealand
New Work Studio

House area: 2260 square feet/210 square meters
Site area: 5705 square feet/530 square meters
Materials: exterior: rusted sheet steel, recycled weatherboard, plywood, polycarbonate sheet, timber joinery; interior: MDF linings, polished concrete floor, timber floor, recycled timber beams and posts, recycled timber stair

The house is located on the southern shoreline of Wellington. Formally, the design for the house is an interplay of spaces and surfaces, allowing an open interconnectedness of spaces at all levels, both vertically and horizontally. Space is a sense of room, of place. Space is also that which sits between materials: the space between floorboard and joist, between joist and wall, between wall and roof, between one lining sheet and another. These spaces are given visibility.

The element of time is an important theme in the house. The reuse of materials both from this site and from others, connects this construction with past places and past uses. The recycled materials are left to retain the patina of their past life; the oil stains on floorboards, the peeling paint on weatherboards, the grease stains and bolt holes on beams and posts, the tin solder on copper sinks. These and other materials are left to continue wearing and weathering. Outside, the weathering is accelerated in the extreme environment—paint peeling, timber silvering, steel rusting. The harshness of the environment is admitted and accepted. In addition, time is expressed as a work-in-progress, by exposed construction—from posts and beams to joists and studs, with lining joints and fixings highlighted, showing the time it takes to make things—and by a present actual finishing that involves a continual reappraisal and reworking of design details.

The house was built for the architect and his young family. The house needed to be robust both indoors and out, with an open and relaxed atmosphere. The house needed to make a statement about the architect Tim Nees' work, to be to a certain extent, a show-home for his business. The challenge was the exposed coastal environment with the solution being accepting change and decay. The result is a kind of hybrid, corrupted modernism, working within a formal framework but also questioning that framework. The craft of building and care with detailing is also evident throughout. The architect's work has been previously described as 'crafted pacific abstraction.'

The house has won several New Zealand Institute of Architects awards, including the prestigious National Award for Architecture in 1999.

Residence and Atelier

Umyeon-dong, Seoul, South Korea
Kim Young-Sub + Kunchook-Moonhwa Architect Associates

House area: 2885 square feet/268 square meters
Site area: 3638 square feet/338 square meters
Materials: reinforced concrete, exposed concrete

Umyeon-dong Choi's residence is located on the side of a road, without a wall; the owner is able to converse through a kitchen window with neighbors or passers-by. If a new neighbor builds a house similar to it on the adjacent site, the two neighbors will be able to open their kitchen windows, and converse. If the gate is open, the house is integrated with the yard as well as the road. Because the yard can be united with the road, it can be said that the house has a sense of communiality.

The house has an atelier used by its owner, a sculptor. The house can be combined with the yard to provide an exhibition space for the owner's sculpture works; in the future, it could be used as his memorial house. If the front and rear windows of the living room are opened, the wind can pass through the room from the backyard, to shake the birch trees planted in the front yard. A wooden terrace annexed to the small kitchen is an attractive area for outdoor entertaining. The porch is adjacent to the pilotis. The owner's recent sculpture works can be exhibited in turn in the pilotis space.

On stepping inside the house, one is faced with three routes; to the living room, to the guest restroom, and to the kitchen. The stairway leading to the bedrooms on the second floor is always closed off from the basement by a door, which is also used as a shoe storage area. The landscape of Mount Umyeon is visible upon reaching the second floor. A guest room lies beyond a wooden deck. The guest room is linked, via an annexed stairway, to the reading room, which in turn is annexed to the atelier on the first floor. Each bedroom on the second floor has a long, horizontal window that frames a picturesque landscape.

Residence at Sanur Elok

Jakarta, Indonesia
Paramita Abirama Istasadhya, PT (PAI)

House area: 8073 square feet/750 square meters
Site area: 11,840 square feet/1100 square meters

The residence was conceived as two building masses grouped together with a small pavilion armature, around a rear pool courtyard. Each building mass is given emphasis as a single component by façade treatments and a mixture of raised and lowered roof structures. The effect is a community of tightly knit components which presents a complementary street façade to the exterior and a reduced scale for the internal court.

Interior spaces are layered, progressing from formal to familiar while circulating around the pool area. On the opposite path to the family areas, the pavilion is sited as a visual terminus for the two-story family room, giving the viewer a sense of oasis in a typical housing tract. Family spaces are left open both horizontally and vertically. The breakfast table has exposure to an intimate corner pool while remaining adjacent to the sitting area. The pantry is open by way of a serving counter and is complete with a work table in a bay window niche. Ground-level floors are finished in polished Italian marble, and the walls are hand-rendered plaster.

Garage and service areas have been located in an open semi-basement to conserve land area for gardens, effectively making the residence three levels. This approach zones servant quarters nearby, while allowing privacy both for the owners and staff. The 1080-square-foot (100-square-meter) master bedroom suite on the second level has a raised bed area, walk-in dressing room, bay-window bath, and sitting room in a sun-filled enclosed terrace, overlooking the rear pool court. Ceilings are of beamed whitewashed oak, floors are beech wood. The suite also benefits from sun exposure from a front facing arched terrace.

Residence for a Sculptor 3

Santa Rosa, California, USA
Sander Architects

House area: 4380 square feet/407 square meters
Site area: 4.5 acres/1.8 hectares

Residence for a Sculptor 3 presents itself frontally on a hillside site, and projects itself consciously as a series of polemics:

Facade/Face versus Viscera/Musculature: a smooth, taut façade is lifted above the hillside and reflects the linear displacement of spaces within. Supporting this is a steel frame and heavier masses, which anchor the house to the ground and are exposed on the rear, uphill side. The dialog here is between fineness and unrefined, between an outward effortless presentation and the internal efforts that are demanded to present this.

Choreography and Expectation: first views of the house advertise a horizontal arrangement and the inference of a view. One enters from behind on the uphill side, away from the suggested view. If expectations promise horizontal and outward, the reality is an inward-focused, strongly vertical entry space where the owner's pottery is on display. This space has a 22-foot (7-meter) curving, torqued steel wall on one side and a curved staircase and wall on the other. Only after venturing through this space, up the stairs and across a bridge does the long view of the Valley of the Moon reveal itself.

Vessel: the entry space, twisting and torqued, dark, vertical, inward, is based on qualities of the owner's large clay pots, a few of which are visible at the base of the stairs. From the inception of the project, the strength of these sculptural clay forms was a deep influence on the making of spaces within the house.

Display/Advertising: the entry vessel and the upstairs great room are conceived as spaces to display the sculptor's work. This sense of demonstration of wares, or offering, allows the house to take a certain pride in the fruits of labors performed there.

Residence on Valentine Creek
Crownsville, Maryland, USA
Good Architecture

House area: 8400 square feet/780 square meters
Site area: 160,000 square feet/14,860 square meters
Materials: wood frame construction with painted gypsum board and stained wood paneling on interior, natural stone, stained wood drop siding, vertical board-and-batten on exterior

From forest to farm to resort to summer haven to suburb, the Chesapeake tidewater region is home to a rich but disappearing heritage of leisure architecture with diverse characteristics. The years after the Civil War brought rapid prosperity to America and the shores of the Chesapeake Bay were dotted with Victorian amusement resorts reached by steamship and rail from Washington and Baltimore. The early years of the automobile saw the rise of romantic waterfront summer colonies such as Sherwood Forest with its green Adirondack-styled cottages; Scientist's Cliffs with its tradition of small chestnut log cabins; and Piney Point on the Potomac River with its graceful arc of sandy beach, Victorian gazebos, and screened sleeping porches.

This new summer and weekend house for a family of four recalls the inherited architectural genetics of the region's casual summer camp traditions. Sited on a very slender ridge surrounded by Valentine Creek and forested parkland near Annapolis, Maryland, the project was designed as a series of hybrid rustic, wood, stone, steel, and glass structures intended to evoke the feeling of a rural camp while serving as a contemporary domestic retreat. A thoughtfully composed arrival sequence controls the movement through the spaces carefully unfolding both water and woodland views. The sequence begins by entering through a narrow 'dogtrot' between two small garages which then emerges onto a light-washed boardwalk overlooking a grass courtyard with a controlled glimpse of the water beyond. Arrival at the entry foyer continues the choreography of water views within the house, while the main living room with its floor-to-ceiling steel windows reveals and frames the ultimate long water view and natural context of the creek.

Reynolds Residence
Western Australia, Australia
Iredale Pedersen Hook Architects

House area (original): 915 square feet/85 square meters; extension area: 1400 square feet/130 square meters
Site area: 10,890 square feet/1012 square meters
Materials: floor: concrete on fill; walls: rendered masonry, sand finished render and steel trowel finished render, lapped recycled jarrah joists, split and nailed on CCA pine framing as wall cladding, Victorian ash panelling, Zincalume custom orb profile; doors: clear anodized aluminum, jarrah and steel framed; windows: jarrah; roof: steel purlins, Zincalume custom orb

This design explores traditional West Australian concepts of domestic architecture, including the spatial possibilities of the lean-to and the Bullnose verandah. Here, the lean-to is longer than the original house and eventually 'leans back' and finishes in the form of a Bullnose that eventually wraps back and floats above the floor level and deck to offer a shelf and external seat. The sand-finished rendered podium to the extension has been introduced to connect the limestone podium of the original house both visually and physically.

The new spaces have been designed as a contrast to the existing introverted spaces. In keeping with the clients' desire for a large, open, light space, large areas of glass and light Victorian ash timber flooring are used. Standard detailing has been incorporated as well as pragmatic structural systems. Materials have been selected for contextual, ecological and economic reasons and for their suitability to perform the desired outcome, and include rendered brick on the curved walls and Bullnose Zincalume on the roof and wall. Recycled jarrah boarding and CCA pine decking have been used both as a suitably ecological and economical material.

Spaces have been organized for solar gain and cross ventilation, reducing the requirement for artificial heating, cooling and lighting. Inexpensive and low-energy light fittings have been used. This is a house for now and in 30 years' time. Materials have been selected on the basis of their transformation over time. The white rendered walls will darken and stain and eventually merge in appearance with the sand-finished rendered podium, the jarrah will soften in color and turn a silky grey, the Zincalume will mellow and soften.

Awards: 2002 Royal Australian Institute of Architects WA Chapter Architecture Award: BHP Steel Award; 2002 Royal Australian Institute of Architects WA Chapter Architecture Award: Archicentre Renovation Award; 2002 Royal Australian Institute of Architects WA Chapter Commendation Award: Alterations and Additions Award; 2002 Australian Institute of Steel Construction High Commendation Award for Metal Building Design.

Ruskin Place Townhouse
Seaside, Florida, USA
Alexander Gorlin Architects

House area: 2000 square feet/186 square meters
Site area: 2000 square feet/186 square meters

The house was conceived both as a critique of the architectural style that developed at Seaside, and an affirmation of its urban code. The abstract, although detailed vocabulary of the house confronts the pseudo-Victorian cottage style of Seaside, as well as the classicism of the townhouses of Ruskin Place, a pedestrian plaza on axis with the center of Seaside. However, it completely conforms to the restrictions of the urban code, including the height restrictions and required balcony. The ground floor is required to be rented as a shop or as an office for arts-related activities.

In some ways, the uniform urban fabric of traditional styles recalls (very distinctly), Paris of the 1920s, ready for the emergence of modernism. A corner unit, the house opens up on the diagonal to Ruskin Place. It also faces a small, forested public park. The public gesture of an open stair leading to the living area above the shop recalls both the open loggias of Italian houses onto a piazza as well as the traditional brownstone stoop, a place for public interaction. The double-height glass cube of the living area both frames a view of the square, and is an intermediary zone between the public space and the internal private realm. An internal façade is created facing the living area, behind which the master bedroom opens out to a terrace facing west.

Rustic Canyon Residence
Santa Monica, California, USA
A C Martin Partners

House area: 6000 square feet/557 square meters
Materials: plaster, concrete, river rock, frosted glass, granite, ebonized maple, maple, Carrara marble

A family needed a compound to house three generations, as well as a peaceful and tranquil living environment. The site is a natural wooded landscape with a large slope that would have a great impact on any design. The architects designed the residence with two dominant themes: order and context. In terms of order, the residence is organized into three elements: the main house, an apartment residence, and the pool house/office. It has a clear, open, flowing circulation throughout, with its high-ceilinged living area, signaled inside and out by an arched window that caps floor-to-ceiling glass. The house is carefully planned in conjunction with the gardens.

The residence includes lower courses, walls, and a ramp of concrete as well as river rock, which is similar to rock found naturally on the site. Built into the hillside to fit harmoniously with the site, it is gently outlined by existing trees and curves to the shape of the land. It features angled roof lines that also mesh with the natural angle of the hill, and makes creative use of trellis and latticed sun-screens to emulate the effect of sunlight through leaves and trees. The residence's upper sections are wood panels; roofs are metal. Exterior walkways are of decomposed granite, extending and complementing the main house's smooth, abstracted concrete exterior. The whole composition's regal elegance is playfully accented by latticed sunscreens that project fan-like from the roofline and especially by a high lookout post accessed by a spiral staircase off the living room.

The residence earned an American Institute of Architects San Fernando Valley Chapter Merit Award in 2000.

Santa Ana House
Santa Ana, Costa Rica
Arquitectura y Diseño SCGMT

House area: 9670 square feet/900 square meters
Materials: concrete block with stucco finish (exterior); mud tiles (roof); external floors in stamped concrete; concrete block with matte paint finish (interior); interior floors in ceramic tile and wood; all doors in solid laurel wood

The owner of the Santa Ana residence is an important banker and politician in Costa Rica, and his social activities include dinner parties and receptions. Based on this, we designed the house around the central patio that includes the swimming pool, jacuzzi and gazebo. Another key point is having the pool as a focal point, visible from all parts of the house. Glass archways in the rooms and hallways allow one to view the central patio with the pool and let natural lighting into the whole house. The owner wanted the house to be well defined and organized. The maid's service area and the garage space were placed on one side of the residence while all private areas and bedrooms are on the other side. The social spaces were organized around the central patio, joining the former two areas. The main lobby is located in the middle of the house, allowing free circulation, without disrupting private spaces.

A very important aspect that influenced the design was the climate. The weather is dry and warm in the summer and very wet during the rainy season, causing high humidity. The best response to this was to open up the house with cross-ventilation in all areas, running throughout the pool area. We utilized the heights to create a more comfortable climate inside the house. To create unique spaces, we chose to have different heights resulting in very interesting volumes inside and outside the residence. It is precisely this dynamic combination of volumes that makes the project stand out from the general mass of houses that surrounds it.

As part of the architectonic language taken from our culture, we designed a house that used classical colonial elements. For this, we emphasized the use of typical building materials used in the Spanish colonial times throughout Central America. Some of these materials include hand-made clay tiles used on the roof, wooden beams, floors, and doors combined with iron window frames. Finally, one of the most symbolic aspects taken from our colonial heritage was the basic design concept of our project: the central patio distribution plan, typical of Spanish Colonial architecture.

Screened House
Fire Island Pines, New York, USA
Bromley Caldari Architects

House area: 2050 square feet/190 square meters
Site area: 14,537 square feet/1350 square meters
Materials: wood frame structure, cedar exterior and interior cladding, corrugated metal exterior cladding, brick tile and oak plank interior flooring, exterior cedar wood deck, timber structure and metal screening at screened-in porch

A narrow wooded lot on the Great South Bay in the resort community of Fire Island Pines is the site for this complete beach house renovation. The existing single-story house was a small, dark box divided into a 'front' and 'back' by a bearing wall/fireplace with dark and cramped bedrooms. There was no sense of the beach or the sea from the existing house.

Creating an envelope for entertaining and socializing as well as a contemplative space for pondering the changing sea and the sun were the main objectives of the renovation. The front portion of the existing house was razed and rebuilt as a double-height, bright and open living/dining space leading to a double-height screened wall and roof porch opening onto the bay beyond. The construction of the house juxtaposes the use of playful and classic materials not normally associated with the beach—brick for floors and roofing tin for wall cladding. The structural frame of 12x12-inch timber columns and wood glue-laminated beams allows for large unbroken spaces and uninterrupted views toward the water. The back (bedroom area) was reconfigured and renovated with new bathrooms, windows and finishes. A new 400-square-foot (37-square-meter) painter's studio was created opposite the existing pool. The studio is circular-shaped and rendered in timber construction and cedar siding. A large garage-type roll-up door completely opens the studio onto the pool deck.

Serrana House
Minas Gerais, Brazil
João Diniz Arquitetura Ltda

House area: 3875 square feet/360 square meters
Site area: 10,800 square feet/1003 square meters
Materials: metallic structure, masonry, tile, quartz stone for floors, wood floors, glass and aluminum for frames, thermo-acoustic roof tiles

The third-largest city in Brazil, Belo Horizonte, 310 miles (500 kilometers) from the Atlantic coast, is the site of this lovely house. The property is inside a preservation area and has an inclination of more than 45 degrees. The mythical 'tree house' finds its expression in this house. The strategy of having the house suspended some distance above the earth is very appropriate, the oblique profile of the land shelters the new construction perfectly and the metallic structure emerges as a convenient option.

There is a linear pavilion of three floors, parallel with the level curves where the pillars reach down to touch the soil. The living area seems to float freely to the forest and the surrounding environment. The access bridge also operates as an architrave balancing the complex. The entrance is at street level along with the kitchen, family room and a garage. Half a level below are the veranda and the large living room; below are the service areas. Half a level above the street access, there is a further room defining two heights for the living room. Beyond this is the private area with three bedrooms, open to the veranda over the living room. There is special meaning to this veranda: it can be understood as an 'invented' land, a suspended and open plaza or a virtual and intimate backyard. The stair box reaches all levels, providing a water collector, which supports the house's solar power.

The Serrana House is a metallic 'palafita' (special structure for water houses), a flying residence with trees under it, visited by winds, branches, squirrels, brothers, and friends. It represents a special and proper way to think of the relationship between people, construction and nature.

Sewell Residence
Cedar Lake, Minnesota, USA
Charles R. Stinson Architects

House area: 5500 square feet/511 square meters
Site area: small urban lake lot
Materials: buff Minnesota limestone, black windows, buff stucco, maple floors and cabinets

In architecture, as in classical music, the art is in the composition. For the Minneapolis urban lake home of philanthropists Fred and Gloria Sewell, the blending of architecture and music was not only natural, it was essential in order to reflect the owners' deep passion for the arts. The three-level home, perched on a pie-shaped lot overlooking Cedar Lake, is an exquisite assemblage of 'floating planes.' Horizontal bands of black-metal gutter-covers and vertical black-stained mahogany posts are juxtaposed with exterior walls of golden Minnesota limestone. Vertical wall planes intersect with floating horizontal ceiling planes, adding a sense of human scale to the open, airy, high-ceilinged rooms. The goal was to keep the design simple, so that the light and the view do all the work and the architecture, while pleasing, doesn't call attention to itself.

Tightly wedged on its lot, the house telescopes out from the two-car garage on the street side and the front entrance through the dining room and great room, to a wall of windows with panoramic views of Cedar Lake. Clerestory windows on the north and east walls admit additional light, block out neighboring houses and focus views into the trees. The light-filled great room features an acoustically friendly maple floor. A Minnesota limestone fireplace adds drama and a sculptural quality; one limestone slab floats above the fireplace as the mantel and an equally thick limestone slab rises up from the floor to form the hearth. Glass display shelves angle out from the fireplace and a vertical black-granite post hides the flue. The great room shares the fireplace with the dining room on the south side of the house.

Steps from the dining room, hidden from view by a half-wall of glass block, is the open-plan kitchen. An elevator, laundry room, phone/office center and powder room are located behind the kitchen. The upper level includes a master bedroom and guest bedroom, whose window seats are positioned with views into the trees and toward the lake. The lower level opens onto the yard, with its access to Cedar Lake, and includes a media room, wet bar, guest room/exercise room, bath, office, and practice room.

Simmonds–Yin Residence
Western Australia, Australia
Joe Chindarsi Architect

House area: 1776 square feet/165 square meters
Site area: 3498 square feet/325 square meters
Materials: rendered and painted brickwork, terrazzo tiling, cherry veneer wall paneling, Tasmanian oak stairs, frameless glass balustrading, anodized aluminum window framing, porcelain and glass mosaics, wool carpet, flush plasterboard ceilings, zincalume metal deck roof sheeting in custom orb profile

The dwelling is a double-story residence, comprising three bedrooms, two bathrooms, and upstairs and downstairs living areas facing front and rear courtyards. The challenge was to design a contemporary and uncompromised dwelling on an urban infill site within the existing heritage streetscape. The dwelling as a mask to the street hides the contemporary dwelling behind a more traditional pitch-roofed front. The idea of blurring boundaries between interior and exterior spaces was employed between the big open-plan room at the back and the rear courtyard in an attempt to make these two spaces read and feel as one, thereby creating a larger whole.

A specific request for an uncompromisingly modern design was initially refused on streetscape issues—the street is in a heritage-listed precinct. As strategy for engagement, a 'mask' was developed as the new front, with pitch and façade proportions alluding to the church next door. Screened from the street, the entry into this residence coyly peeks out from the side, slipping past as a slot recessed back to the 'other' side of the house. The foyer is a sliver of a double-height space, which is conceptually continuous with the 'big room' out back.

The dwelling was designed with thermal efficiency in mind. Masonry walls, and concrete slabs result in a high thermal mass, stabilizing internal temperatures between night and day, winter and summer. There are no openings facing south. Openings to the east facing the street allow the morning sun to enter. North-facing glass is protected by an eaves overhang that allows sun to penetrate into the dwelling in winter, but provides protection in summer. To the west, there is extensive glazing due to the connection with the rear courtyard, but a generous eaves overhang, and careful placement of a deciduous tree and high courtyard walls provide protection from the western sun.

The use of cavity brickwork construction in conjunction with structural steel within cavities to support across void areas and stabilize two-story-high walls was chosen because of ease and simplicity of construction. Other materials were chosen for their durability, such as commercial-grade aluminium framing to doors and windows, and quality hardware, tapware and fixtures.

Simplicity

Mustique, St. Vincent and the Grenadines
Diamond and Schmitt Architects Incorporated

House area: 4000 square feet/372 square meters
Site area: 6 acres/2.4 hectares
Materials: plaster over concrete block and concrete, cedar shingle roofing, board ceilings, glass

A three-bedroom house, staff cottage, carport, market garden terraces and swimming pool are situated on a sloping, rocky and well-treed site facing southeast and the ocean. Each room of the small complex is itself a building. These pavilions have been arranged to take advantage of the easterly breeze, and of the panoramic views of the sea and sky, and to provide privacy for each bedroom. In addition to the provision of generous cross-ventilation to every room, all roof spaces are ventilated for cooling. A long retaining wall and courtyard are the elements used to tie the composition together, and give social focus to the house.

The few materials used are plaster over concrete block and concrete, white-painted tray ceilings, cedar shingle roofing, and painted wood shutters. Glazed doors are only used for rain and wind protection in two locations, the southeast face of the living and dining rooms. The exterior plaster color was created by using naturally red Trinidad stone and white cement. The texture was achieved by adding a small proportion of fine stone aggregate to the plaster, and scraping a wood board over semi-dry plaster. Floors are also made of the same plaster mix, without the stone aggregate. Interiors are white-painted plaster finished with a wood trowel.

The natural bush has been reinforced with native frangipani and other tropical flowering and fruit-bearing trees. The courtyards have been planted with yellow and ochre bougainvilleas, thumbergia for the trellises and plumbago in blue clay pots at the swimming pool.

Stabilized Earth Poll House

Margaret River, Western Australia, Australia
Gary Marinko Architects

House area: 3230 square feet/300 square meters
Site area: 25 acres/10 hectares
Materials: stabilized earth, color-stained plywood, Zincalume metal sheets in a Custom Orb profile, fiberglass sheets in a Custom Orb profile, pressed galvanized iron louvers with a baked enamel finish, Western red cedar windows, trowel-finished concrete slab

The site is adjacent to a national park of dense bushland in a wine-growing region. The house has been built with a limited palette of materials; the emphasis is on creating space that is animated by the changing quality of natural light entering through the windows and skylights.

Massive stabilized earth walls reach out to engage the landscape, to mark pathways across the site and through the house, and to primarily form courtyards. The winter courtyard is hard-landscaped with river rocks and paving slabs and is enclosed entirely by buildings. The summer courtyard is shaded by the main roof of the house and has framed views of the distant landscape; its southern wall can be folded back to open up to the main courtyard and to the breeze.

The house orientation and design maximize the entry of the winter sun; it is naturally ventilated. An internal stabilized earth wall divides the living and sleeping areas on the north from the service areas on the south. A continuous skylight illuminates all these service rooms and allows diffuse light from the hall to balance the brighter northern glazing. The living spaces have large framed views of the landscape to the north and into the winter courtyard. These spaces can be transformed to an introverted space by the closure of a series of shutters that change both the quality and quantity of the light and the shape of the rooms. The separate studio, in contrast to the house, is tall and dark-colored, an internalized, contemplative environment lined completely in plywood with all its service areas concealed, with most of its natural light coming through the roof.

Steinhardt Residence

Birmingham, Michigan, USA
McIntosh Poris Associates

House area: 3500 square feet/325 square meters
Materials: industrial cinder block, metal decking, steel trusses, sea wall, maple floor, limestone fireplaces, soapstone counters, marble counters

The program included a ground up, three-level house with two porches (one screened-in) and a private terrace. The first floor includes a living room, kitchen, dining area, 'keeping' room (sitting area near kitchen), and a powder room. The second floor includes the master bedroom, master bathroom, and a home office. On the basement level there are two guest bedrooms, a guest bathroom, and an exercise room.

This very contemporary house is set amongst more traditional homes from the 1920s. The initial concept was to build a loft as a single-family home. The result—an urban townhouse—is very open with minimal intervention in the space. Storage areas are either hidden or used as room dividers. As well, as an individual house, the clients get much more light than would

normally be available in a multi-tenant loft building. The steel-framed house has concrete floors with radiant heat (maple on the second floor), exposed metal deck, steel trusses, limestone fireplaces, soapstone counters, aluminum-framed commercial windows, and exterior simulated stone blocks. Sea wall—usually used on piers—is used for the retaining wall. The architects worked with the client (an interior designer) to integrate all the materials, interior finishes, and furnishings. Several levels are at play, with the master suite overlooking the living room, and a subterranean terrace, which the owner refers to as her 'Soho terrace'. Although the house is on a corner lot, with lots of windows, it still affords the owner a sense of privacy.

Studio House

Seattle, Washington, USA
Olson Sundberg Kundig Allen Architects

House area: 7200 square feet/669 square meters
Site area: 35,000 square feet/3,251 square meters
Materials: concrete, steel, lead-coated copper

The Studio House occupies a heavily wooded neighborhood, on a point of land along a bluff overlooking Puget Sound. A close friend of the client lived in the house previously on the site, and she wanted to remember that friend in her own dwelling. Its design incorporates these vestigial memories in a new form: fragments and geometries from the prior home appear throughout the property, serving to recall the earlier inhabitant.

The new plan is laid over that of the old one, turned 13 degrees to take better advantage of views. Entry is through a two-story steel lantern placed between the foundation wall of the old house and the walls of the new one. The primary interior volume is a two-story space used both as the main living area and as a photographic studio. It captures the outdoors through a large open west wall that incorporates shading devices when needed. The bold structural steel frame and the concrete walls are left raw, and allowed to age naturally to show the passage of time. A curved roof diffuses natural and artificial ambient light. An armature of unfinished steel cantilevers over the room to accommodate general room lighting, fans, and studio lighting. Open metal stairs and landings align with the old and new geometries.

At one end of this main space, a tall box contains the kitchen and pantry below, and bedrooms and baths above. Conceived as a cabinet, its upper floor projects like an open drawer and is purposely left in a raw state of finish. At the other end, a photo workroom and office form a second inserted volume. Heavy concrete perimeter walls wrap the building protectively on three sides. The curved roof and garage rooftop structures are covered in subtly reflective lead-coated copper.

Sunrise Road House

Palm Beach, New South Wales, Australia
Dawson Brown Architecture

House area: 2690 square feet/250 square meters
Site area: 15,790 square feet/1467 square meters
Materials: timber, stone, corrugated iron

This heritage project involved the restoration/renovation and pavilion additions to a 'Craftiness Timber Bungalow' designed by James Peddle in 1916. The building had been untouched since 1921 and presented many problems, including poor physical condition, tiny scale and the difficulty of extending/modernizing such a building while preserving its unique character.

Built of random stone, unframed board-and-batten timber walls, with a corrugated iron roof, this minimal construction technique provides a lasting testament to the appropriate use of timber and its environmental compatibility over time. The original house was severely affected by white-ant attack in parts and was carefully dismantled with affected timbers being repaired and replaced, maintaining all the original fabric. The well-documented original drawings and the restoration work allowed the builder to become immersed in the building techniques used 80 years ago.

The new design is a deliberate, sensitive, heritage-based solution, seeking minimal change to the original house by providing additional accommodation in pavilion form. The careful siting of the addition, the small relative scale and subtle connection to the original, maintains the dominance of the early house in relation to the original. The new additions were seen very much as outbuildings, just like country properties, which have rambling collections of structures to the rear of the main house. A resulting problem was that the entry now was via the rear, hence the concept of a boardwalk linking the new to the old.

The dividing up of the brief into two buildings, one long, the other high, created the sense of passage between them, a fragmentation of the form to conceal the original, yet reveal it as one moves along the boardwalk. While the buildings never touch, the sense of enclosure is everywhere. Materials are similar in the new work but detailing is clearly contemporary, allowing for the architectural story to be read by the observer. This is a place not so much about architecture, but a home, a place for the soul created out of timber by craftsmen in 1916 and 2000, craftsmen of equal passion sharing an innate understanding of the materials of their craft.

Swatt House

Lafayette, California, USA
Swatt Architects

House area: 3600 square feet/335 square meters
Detached studio area: 400 square feet/37 square meters
Site area: 1.5 acres/0.6 hectare
Materials: wood frame over concrete pier and grade beam foundation, integral color stucco, cedar board siding, custom mahogany doors and windows, terrazzo, hardwood and carpet flooring, painted gypsum board walls, exposed Douglas fir glu-laminated beams, exposed hemfir decking, cedar soffits, birch cabinets, birch and mahogany doors, precast concrete countertop and fireplace surround

This project is an architect's own home for a family of five including three young children in Lafayette, California (approximately 20–25 miles east of San Francisco). The residence is situated on a north-facing site, overlooking a creek, mature oak trees, and the hills of Briones Regional Park beyond. The design takes advantage of the rural views to the north, while maximizing natural daylight from the south. Exterior spaces, including a swimming pool, two terraces, and a south-facing entry courtyard, have been designed to promote a strong connection to the natural environment.

The interior of this house is organized around a glazed, south-facing, two-story spine, which serves to reinforce circulation, admit maximum daylight, and provide access to the entry courtyard. Five bi-folding glass doors open the spine and living areas to the entry courtyard, virtually eliminating the separation between indoor and outdoor space.

The internal organization of the house is expressed on the exterior by material changes. Horizontal cedar board siding and mitered glass enclose the spine and contrast with the integral colored stucco skin of the main living spaces. In form, the house is quiet, restrained and modern, building on the language of earlier modern West Coast architecture.

Sweet Pond

Lunenburg, Nova Scotia, Canada
Diamond and Schmitt Architects Incorporated

House area: 4000 square feet/372 square meters
Site Area: 25 acres/10 hectares
Materials: cedar clapboard, cedar shingle roofs, double-hung sash windows, 12-inch pine boards, cherry battens

Rock, pine, an indented coastline, and indigenous blueberry and cranberry characterize the landscape. When purchased in 1995 the property had one structure—a cedar shingle salt box with sliding-sash wood windows and a small boathouse. Sweet Pond is now a complex of six similar structures with cedar clapboard, cedar shingle roofs and double-hung sash windows. These structures are arranged around a well-defined herb garden court with pebble paths, and loosely around a garden court. Each structure has an iron stove made by the Lunenburg Foundry. The walls on the interior are lined with 12-inch pine boards and horizontal cherry battens. The detailing is in the Lunenburg tradition.

The seventh structure is a summer house, which has a sod roof over log beams, a fireplace and chimney made from stone from the cove and a frame enclosure of glass and insect screening. The composition is tied together and to the landscape with cedar decks and paths. Buildings, windows and doorways frame views of the landscape. Bisecting this composition is a central axis of movement—drive shed for arrival by car to the west, boathouse for arrival by sea on the east.

The Butcher Ranch

Gonzales County, Texas, USA
Michael G. Imber, Architect

House area: 2867 square feet/266 square meters
Materials: painted plaster, redwood siding, antique oak wood lintels salvaged from owner's ranch, redwood frame porch, Oklahoma sandstone flagstone flooring, standing seam metal roof, painted mahogany wood windows and doors, long-leaf pine plank ceiling, Texas cordova limestone carved stone lintel at fireplace, painted wood plank siding, custom-designed wrought-iron chandeliers

The interior of the Butcher Ranch is a simple expression of the different elements of the structure. Thick exterior walls are hand-troweled sheetrock to emulate plaster over stone. Interior walls are expressly infill, constructed out of wood—thin and sheathed in painted 1x wood material to express a common interior substrate used prior to the advent of gypsum board. This also lends the stair (the primary dividing element between the living and sleeping quarters) a hardy outdoor quality. The master bedroom lacks a closet, the client instead opting for two traditional built-in armoires on each side of the bed.

The wood saddle on the north side of the house accommodates modern functions such as kitchen, laundry, and entry. The ceiling in these areas is of simple 1x6 over 2x4 long-leaf pine. An opening through the thick white wall is further expressed as exterior envelope by a remnant transom overhead, matching the other exterior doors. The main living space is

shielded at the entry by a furniture-like cabinet that accommodates both coat closet at the entry, and pantry at the kitchen. The kitchen works within the main living space, but is unobtrusively tucked behind an island and into the adjacent shed.

The main living space is full-height, taking in the dormers that serve as windows for the guest room on the other side of the house. The small windows on the entry side of the house help accommodate the owner's art collection, while glass doors opposite open onto the screened porch. The space is anchored on one end by the large fireplace with an intricately carved native limestone mantle. The ceiling is of simple long-leaf pine with panels laid across the exposed collar ties, leaving space above the collar ties for mechanical equipment.

The client's family background in shipping and his love of wooden boat building drove the overall concept of the house. The small windows in the austere mass shine as portals at night. The clean German aesthetic works well for the compartmentalized interiors—every function has its place in the small house with the bathrooms and mechanicals tucked into the bulkhead separating the two major components of the house. The minimal woodwork is just enough to warm the interiors for comfort.

The Haven

Upper Brookfield, Queensland, Australia
Paul Uhlmann Architects

House area: 3230 square feet/300 square meters
Site area: 10 acres/4 hectares
Materials: timber board cladding, concrete block, steel, timber floor, timber truss roof

The Haven is a permanent residence, designed as a retreat from the hustle and bustle of daily city work life. Located at Upper Brookfield, the residents are transported on a daily basis to a place of peace and serenity. The house is a single platform which, when inside, allows the residents above the natural understory yet to be shaded by the upper canopy. The platform allows views of neighboring forests and distant ridgelines. The house is divided into distinct living and sleeping zones by a central kitchen and outdoor living spaces. The hallway acts as a spine for the building with all rooms branching from this axis. The length of the building runs parallel with the contours of the site; this orientation attaches the building to the topography of the site. A lounge area that acts as a retreat from the wilderness has been created to the rear of the house. The residence was sited as far as practical from the road to provide as much privacy as possible. To enhance the arrival to the house and to detach the house further from the public road, the user has to meander down the driveway. The front elevation of the house is dominated by a sweeping arc, creating a dramatic contrast with the natural bush setting. The use of this short elevation at such an angle, softens the actual length and size of the building.

The Point House

Montana, USA
Bohlin Cywinski Jackson

House area: 2200 square feet/204 square meters
Site area: 20 acres/8 hectares
Materials: cedar siding, copper roof, Cor-ten steel siding, copper-clad wood windows, structural steel, board-formed concrete, maple cabinetry

Set on a peninsula that extends into a large western Montana lake, this house is part of a year-round family compound and was conceived as both the hub of daytime activities and a quiet retreat for the family's head.

Consisting primarily of untouched forest and wetlands that flank the peninsula, the site called for a delicate intervention that maintained the unspoiled natural beauty of the land, while allowing access and enjoyment in a rugged climate with extreme seasons. Sliding between cedars and pines on the secluded point, the house extends from the rock spine to the edge of the dense wetlands. A long linear wall of Cor-ten steel slices through the site and organizes the various building elements. On the northern face, two boxes clad in heavy cedar planks house bathrooms and utilities. The living spaces face south to the lake and open onto a wood deck running the length of the house. The edge separating the inside from the landscape is intentionally blurred with tall walls of glass and large sliding panels.

Rigorous in detail and delicate in spirit, this house is a pavilion under the trees and a platform on the land, dedicated to both gatherings and contemplative moments.

The Red House

Oslo, Norway
Jarmund / Vigsnæs AS Architects

House area: 1830 square feet/170 square meters
Site area: 10,760 square feet/1000 square meters

Materials: rendered insulated concrete block (base), wooden structure, 200mm insulation, wooden cladding; corrugated steel plates on glulam beams (roof structure); double-glazed, heat-reflecting windows; painted plasterboard, painted wooden paneling (walls); American ash floor (top floor), sandstone (ground floor)

The site for the house is a former garden on the east bank of a heavily wooded river valley in the western suburbs of Oslo. Despite the site's suburban context, the surrounding fir and pine trees offer seclusion and provide the illusion that the residence lies somewhere more remote. The building is placed perpendicular to the stream, to heighten the dramatic potential of the setting and to avoid obstructing the view for the house beyond.

The house is organized on two floors. Living spaces and the parents' bedroom are on the top (entry) floor, oriented towards the south and the view, culminating in a covered terrace among the trees to the west. The lower floor houses the children's bedrooms and a family room, facing the river valley to the north. This double orientation is the basis for the architectonic dynamic of the project, and the design is in all dimensions focused on enhancing this theme.

In a country that experiences freezing temperatures and short daylight hours during winter, lighting was an important factor in the building design. Trees surround the north and west façades, so extensive fenestration wraps much of the house in order to maximize natural lighting to the interior. The vibrant red color of the building's stained wood exterior is a striking feature, in contrast with its frosty setting.

The Water House

Sydney, New South Wales, Australia
Dale Jones-Evans Pty Ltd

House area: 3230 square feet 300/square meters
Site area: 1990 square feet 185/square meters
Materials: painted cement render, natural slate and metal deck roof, traditional timber and galvanized steel windows, aluminum rod artists screen, white quartz, sandstone, bluestone, dark polished timber floors, stucco and white laminated glass walls, dark-stained recycled timber, steel stair, painted plasterboard ceilings, white glass walls, limestone floors, white glass tiles, honed Carrara marble basins (bathrooms), dark stained and polished timber with stainless steel (kitchen)

The design gesture for The Water House was simple: to ensure the new inserted architecture eliminated any sense of being in a terrace typology while maintaining some memory of the former terrace. This was achieved by gutting the building, maintaining only the perimeter walls and street façade. Light quality, both received and transmitted, and the presence of water were equally critical to the transformation process. Internally, a remnant of a former front room is maintained and leads to a steel chassis, which marches its way through and out of the terraced envelope, taking full expression within the building. A powerful spatial gesture, an inverted T-form, reorganizes the internal mechanics and space planning of the former terrace. The ground plan is open, and a dramatic three-story light-scoop atrium illuminates the space by day and acts as an illumination core by night. A basement was also added.

An uncompromised re-making of a former terrace to ensure that light, openness and human comfort were optimized was the simple, practical and functional strategy. However poetic and artistic desires of suggesting 'a façade and the other', 'to maintain a remnant memory while carefully walking away from it', 'to suggest other spaces exist without revealing them at once' and to arrive at these aesthetic notions through a re-technologized row house were paramount.

The material conduct and orchestration of the building grows off a raw palette. The internal floor planes of dark timber ground you, the stair floats on steel above water, the walls are reflective gallery receptors (plaster finish) and the interior hangs on its new steel skeleton. The external expression moves from a reinvigorated historicism (the street façade), it travels through nothingness (the western glass and steel chassis), returns to the idea of weight (the stone court), and terminates on the suggestion of 'beyond', behind the light aluminium veil a black pool of water.

Tivoli Road Residence

Melbourne, Victoria, Australia
Jan Manton Design Architecture

House area: 3230 square feet/300 square meters
Site area: 4392 square feet/408 square meters
Materials: white render, recycled timber posts and beams, natural anodized aluminum louvers and window frames, bluestone paving

The site is located in an inner suburb of Melbourne, within a heritage overlay with a double-fronted Victorian house on the south boundary. The arrangement of the buildings on the site is reminiscent of a typical Victorian residential site where the main bulk of the house is located at the front of the block with garage and out-buildings to the rear of the block. In this case, the garage is linked to the house by a covered external walkway.

The house contains six rooms in total plus external spaces related to the living areas. The ground floor living/entertaining area is essentially one large space with a stair and service core separating the living, dining and entrance spaces. A galley kitchen and bar are located off the dining room to the west. A series of courtyard gardens surrounds the house to the north, east and west. The first floor has three rooms: two bedrooms both with ensuites, a laundry and a long study which is designed to be split in half, providing a house with three bedrooms and study if required.

The north elevation reveals a floating, rectangular first-floor mass supported by two bookend 'blocks'. The view from the front of the house expresses these blocks as a group of receding rectangular forms proportioned to mimic the façades of the neighboring double-fronted Victorian houses in the street. A projecting window seat protruding from the first floor mass extends almost its full length, internally linking the two bedrooms and study. These windows, when open, slide over each other providing the first-floor rooms with an inside/outside aspect.

Tonn Residence

Dash Point, Washington, USA
Anderson Anderson Architecture

House area: 4742 square feet/440 square meters (living area); 5938 square feet/552 square meters (built area)
Site area: 33,728 square feet/3133 square meters
Materials: wood and steel structure, stucco and steel siding, Douglas fir interior paneling, concrete floors

The Tonn house is a fairly simple, T-shaped organization of interior spaces, arranged to form an entry court at the back of the house and a partially contained living deck on the view side of the house facing northwest, where the summer sun sets behind the Olympic mountain range. The house is primarily one big, slightly twisted continuous room, with defined functional areas oriented according to favorable relationships to the sun and views.

Sitting on a high bank above Puget Sound, surrounding trees accentuate the inward focus of the gently dished slope, so that the house appears to sit in a distinct trough, following the fall line of the hill. The roof of the house bends into a shallow 'V', paralleling the cross-slope dish of the hillside. At the same time, the longitudinal axis of the roof folds downward to follow the hill, slumping into a comfortable resting position on the earth, not statically resisting its position, but flowing into the implied motion of the site.

The roof is the most important element of this house—a warm wooden cloud weighing in on the interior, defining a space between the sloping land and the heavy sky. This is a very characteristic Northwest experience: living on a hillside under a heavy sky, light poking in horizontally at sunrise and sunset, creating spectacular moments at the horizon, reflecting richly off the ceiling of clouds. Sometimes during the day, a hole opens up and the light pours in from the middle of the sky. This roof works in the same way, with its central dormer angling toward the southeastern sky, bringing light over its shoulder, deep into the house.

Tree House, Studio – Pavilion

Palm Beach, New South Wales, Australia
Dawson Brown Architecture

Tree House area: 410 square feet/38 square meters
Site area: 1615 square feet/150 square meters
Materials: timber, stone, copper

This 1920's, local council heritage-listed cottage is located on the ridge line at Palm Beach, north of Sydney. Straddling two blocks, the site has an eastern aspect facing the Pacific Ocean on a steep slope providing a very private reserve. The project involved refurbishment and repair of the original timber and stone cottage, new accommodation, pool, terraces, and a separate pavilion.

The basement of the existing cottage, built of rustic sandstone in a typical 1920's geometric design, provides sleeping areas. The refurbished upper level, with original black stained timber walls, accommodates new kitchen and living areas. The additions continue the established character by building along the contours of the site and incorporating original materials with contemporary variations in detail. The bushland setting is maintained by minimizing the scale and bulk of new work, and by the introduction of a delicate yet sturdy pavilion, accessed via a bridge spanning the pool. This 'tree house' pavilion with its scissor-truss legs allowed the building to be gently placed among the trees with minimal impact upon the natural rock shelves and established banksias.

The materials used provide subtle telltales as to the layers of history added to this listed building. The rustic, robust character of these early houses is reflected in the exposed structural tectonics of the pavilion addition.

Tugun Towerhouse

Queensland, Australia
Paul Uhlmann Architects

House area: 1940 square feet/180 square meters
Site area: 2175 square feet/202 square meters
Materials: plywood cladding with timber battens, fiber-cement wall cladding, polycarbonate wall sheeting, rendered concrete block, steel, plywood floor

Tugun Towerhouse is perched atop a beach-side hill overlooking the Pacific Ocean. The clients had lived on the site for some years prior to reinventing their place of residence. The result was a three-story tower that optimizes views, orientation and seclusion of the site. Panoramic views of the ocean are maximized by expansive living decks and strategically located windows. Views of neighboring native forests allow for environmental interaction at an intimate scale.

The clients wanted the atmosphere of their home to express its beach-side location, as well as possessing an ambience of sophistication obtained by the contemporary use of materials, planning and architectural aesthetics. The building has a small footprint due to the size restriction of the site. This constraint resulted in the building's height and form, and minimal impact. The materials that have been used are nostalgic of traditional Australian beach house construction. The use of repetition, exaggeration and an unusual use of materials have created an individual beach house design.

Each level of the house consists of sliding panels that create a freedom of use of the spaces. Wall panels in the bathroom retract to allow views while bathing, and panels in the living rooms open to enhance the feeling of living on a platform. This blurring of edges captivates the casual spirit of coastal living.

Victoria Park House

Singapore
SCDA Architects Pte Ltd

House area: 16,039 square feet/561 square meters
Site area: 8923 square feet/829 square meters

Set on steep-sloping terrain, the Victoria Park House occupies a rectangular site that ascends 16 feet (5 meters) from front to rear. Access is through a vehicular entrance court, which leads to a sub-basement garage, while pedestrians ascend via a flight of external stairs that lead to an elevated patio overlooking the driveway.

The accommodation is arranged around a southeast-facing courtyard containing an almost square swimming pool. A two-story, L-shaped block along the long northwest and the short northeast boundaries of the site encloses the court and a single-story glazed pavilion contains the living room on the southwest. Both blocks have shallow monopitch roofs clad in profiled steel. A wide corridor runs the full length of the house, forming a linear axis that is almost in line with the center of the rectangular site. Upon entering the house from the elevated patio, the living pavilion is deployed to the right of this axis. To the left is a circular stairwell that ascends from the garage below. Alongside the stairwell is a spacious, light-filled, two-story dining area. Immediately beyond this are the wet and dry kitchens. Tucked out of site in the northern corner of the house are the mandatory civil defence shelter and other service areas.

The principal staircase to the upper floors terminates the axis. To the right of the staircase are the family room and a guestroom with an external timber deck extending to the edge of the pool. The focus of all the principal rooms is the swimming pool in the courtyard, which has an extension running alongside the southeast site boundary in the form of a lap pool.

Villa Fujii

Kitasaku, Nagano, Japan
Motomu Uno + Keizo Ikemura / Phase Associates

House area: 3434 square feet/319 square meters
Site area: 17,800 square feet/1654 square meters
Materials: larch board, glass, aluminum spandrel, marble, oak, plasterboard, laminated Douglas fir

The rectangular site is wrapped by widespread trees and bushes. The challenge in designing a house was to incorporate this environment into the building. The step-by-step process was: set reinforced concrete slabs away from the ground on each level; draw a zigzag walkway extending throughout the site, wooden decks in each dimension, and a bridge over the walkway; roof-over the reinforced concrete walls with the hybrid structure of wood and steel, organize public and private spaces below the roof; characterize spaces by adapting to each structural system, and crop horizontal/vertical views of interior/exterior by cutting walls off freely; arrange furniture, fittings and structural components as the elements of interior landscape, and feature the combination of materials and lights to enhance the quality of space.

The relationship between nature and architecture was studied carefully with the aim of providing relaxation for the client, and a haven from his daily urban life. By seeing the landscape as visual transmissions on the glass of the windows, the alternate relationship of interior/exterior or artifacts/nature emerged in the contemporary comfort of his second house.

The figure and the form of the house came from the relationship with the landscape, taking into account the local climate (the temperature is 10 degrees lower than Tokyo and the humidity is extremely high), the slight undulations in the ground, and the widespread random pattern of trees such as oaks, cherry trees, and larches. The interior composition also followed this approach by regarding it as a sequence of landscapes. A landscape architect and a structural engineer were also involved in the design from the beginning. The variety of large glass openings and their supports, and the hybrid structural systems showing the volume of space light, were developed throughout the construction.

Waratah Bay House

Walkerville/Waratah Bay, Victoria, Australia
Holan Joubert Architects

House area: 893 square feet/83 square meters (dwelling and laundry/store); 410 square feet/38 square meters (carport undercroft); 140 square feet/13 square meters (suspended deck)
Site area: 2.4 acres/1 hectare
Materials: steel structure, Colorbond roofing, Victorian blackwood hardwood flooring, spotted gum hardwood decking, 1/2-inch (12mm) toughened glass (balustrading)

This project is a coastal house built aloft to its prescribed height limit with panoramic sea views. Poised on just four double I-beam portals, the corners are free to float without immediate support. These corners are further dissolved using butt-jointed glass through two stories. With its double skillion roofs in counterpoint, the ceilings rake up to views of Wilson's Promontory as well as the green pastures inland. As the house is also relatively isolated, it also integrates water collection using the geometry of the house and its roof forms. Its program is basic in terms of habitation: at ground level, there are two water tanks, stairs with laundry underneath and cover for two cars. The first 'platform' is for sleeping (two bedrooms) with one bathroom; the top 'platform' is an open-plan square of living and dining with a projecting balcony.

The steel members were precision-cut and assembled off-site, and constructed on-site like a huge meccano set. Even the innovative steel sun-shades at mid-level were welded to the frame off-site. In turn, a specialized double-glazing system and custom-orb clad stud walls were treated literally like infill panels and efficiently constructed. All exposed faces of the roof are clad in 'gull grey' Colorbond to form a protective shell over the building. The use of Colorbond panels is also extended to the wall cladding, which is clearly expressed in large rectangular panels between the structural beams and expansive glazing on all four elevations. This iconic Australian building material relates to its coastal and semi-rural context.

This general imagery of steel is complemented by ancillary elements fabricated from thermoplastics. The strong opaque volumes of the entry stair and white plastic water tanks contrast with the sharp steel and glass structure. The expression of white plastic to the stair/laundry complex and water tanks adds a new vocabulary to the more conventional vernacular of steel and corrugated iron. Various images familiar to this remote coastal area have been integrated into the expression of this building. These include lifesaver towers, the local lighthouses and the Bass Strait oil rigs. As a coastal metaphor, the image of a seagull with its grey wings and upright stance on thin, red legs also influenced the identity of this lone dwelling.

Weathering Steel House

Toronto, Ontario, Canada
Shim-Sutcliffe Architects

In the Toronto garden suburb of Don Mills, 1960's ranch bungalows and their surrounding landscaping are being levelled, to be replaced by substantial, clumsy, historically referential monster-houses. Constructed of beige brick, taupe-colored stucco and reconstituted stone, these new houses form the new ideal suburban dream house. Complemented by decorative and ornamental landscaping, they are the antithesis of their modernist predecessors.

This residence sits in direct contrast to this context. Materially rich, dark, and abstract, it creates a clear threshold to the world within, to the site it creates and to the ravine edge over which it looks. The L-shaped house frames a reconfigured landscape created around shaped, tree-covered mounds and a sweeping meadow. Imbedding itself into the center of the house, the reflecting pool and swimming pool beyond form the intermediary between building and landscape, weaving reflected light, motion and sound into the heart of the project. From the street, this house is seemingly much more opaque than adjacent buildings—sculptural cut-outs in the elevation offer precise, transparent glimpses of the ravine beyond. Upon entering, a circulation space parallel to the front elevation connects garage entry, front entry, basement courtyard and second floor in one continuous slice of vertical and horizontal space. From the entry, one catches a glimpse of the ravine treetops beyond before rising up a few steps to the main living level.

A skylight and inverted bay window drop a pool of light on the landing of the stair to the second floor, terminating the reflecting pool axis. At the second floor, this inverted bay window and a large window on the south side of the house help to form a bridge-like condition linking the master bedroom and the children's wing.

Webster Residence

Venice, California, USA
Steven Ehrlich Architects

House area: 3600 square feet/335 square meters
Site area: 3660 square feet/340 square meters
Materials: exposed structural moment frame steel, concrete (finished) floor acts as structural slab, wood framing, painted stucco, cement board, roll-up garage glass doors, exposed structural lumber, plywood sub-floor

Located in Venice, California, the Webster Residence utilizes the oasis of an interior courtyard as an antidote to the urban context. Just a half-block from the beach, the rectangular lot fronts a pedestrian street, one of only a handful of streets closed to traffic in Venice. In plan, the building consists of two volumes at each end of the lot, linked by a service spine on the east and the central courtyard complete with a reflecting pool. Moment frame steel I-beams frame roll-up glass doors on the two façades that face the courtyard and the front façade that links to the street. This open axis provides an unparalleled level of open space, with an uninterrupted flow from the ground floor living and dining in the front across the courtyard, and up a flight of steps into a rear studio through another roll-up door. The amphitheater-like steps that rise from the courtyard further enhance this procession of space. The raised platform not only provides an additional vantage to enjoy the exterior, but it also moderates the site's 5-foot (1.5-meter) rise in grade from front to back to allow for a two-car garage at the alley. When all three garage doors are opened, the house transforms itself into a pavilion of connected courts and spaces.

The layout of the house introduces several upper-level terraces and a large roof deck to allow the owner private and public venues to enjoy the views of the Pacific. The general feeling of the house is of complete openness, but with sliding curtains, spaces are transformed into private hideaways largely concealed from public view. The glass roll-up doors on the lower level allow spaces to flow uninterrupted into the exterior, expanding the livable area of the house without constructing additional square footage. The courtyard spaces moderate the warm summer temperatures and provide a comfortable micro-climate through lush plantings and running water. Additionally, normally enclosed rooms such as the bedrooms and studio are opened to the outdoors in a matter of seconds with oversized roll-away windows mounted on the exterior façades, and aluminum-framed sliding doors.

Constant ocean breezes allow for natural ventilation to the point that the house has no air conditioning system. A central heating system was included but is only necessary on the coldest of nights, particularly with the thermal mass the concrete floors provide.

Williams Residence

Marion, Virginia, USA
Kamal Amin Associates

House area: 6000 square feet/557 square meters

The client, Harry Williams, owned the largest prefabricated steel company in the world. He was fascinated by a house in Palm Springs that he had seen published, and which the architect had worked on with a partner a few years earlier.

The fact that the house was built on a rather steep hill suggested a two-level solution with the lower level resting on lower grade. The 360-degree view suggested almost complete round shapes and a two-story structure. The main (upper) level of 4500 square feet (418 square meters) comprises the living room, dining area, library, wet bar, master bedroom complete with large dressing and bath facilities, and two guest suites. The lower level of 1500 square feet (139 square meters) comprises a games room, a sitting room with wet bar, a sauna, hydromassage facility, maid's quarters, off-season storage and a number of bathrooms. A sound system is piped throughout the whole house.

The main building material is local granite exposed inside and out in load-bearing walls. All paneling is cherry scribed to and set in the masonry without trim, thus accentuating the sensuality afforded by the contrast in textures. The heights inside the building vary from 7 feet (2.1 meters) under the decks to 12 feet (3.7 meters) at the center of the domes. The house is large, but spaces resolve into intimate areas with comfortable perceptions. The flow of space from one configuration to the other is unobstructed, thus rooms borrow vistas from each other.

Williers House

Tampa, Florida, USA
John Howey & Associates

House area: 3000 square feet/279 square meters
Site area: 15,000 square feet/1395 square meters
Materials: vertical lapped or shiplapped 1x6 cedar, copper, bronze, cypress decks, tinted glass, acrylic skylight, carpet, drywall, textured marble, ceramic tile

Situated on an in-town wooded lot for a bachelor whose place of business is nearby, this residence was designed with two zones in mind: a public zone, entered from under a bridge to a central two-story living space edged by glass, to a courtyard-enclosed pool with views of surrounding oak trees. At one side is the formal dining room, kitchen, bar and garage. At the other side is a guest bedroom wing. The personal sleeping-recreation zone is situated above the master bedroom, with a dressing and bath wing with a nautilus-inspired shower for two. This zone is connected by the bridge to a large recreation space with a hot tub and exercise equipment at the other end.

Because the residence is located on a corner lot, and to save a large existing oak tree, the structure was turned 45 degrees to its site boundaries. All zoned spaces focus out, with large glass areas, balconies and decks, to the private wall-enclosed landscaped swimming area. Formal entry is to the gallery bordering the living space with a circular stair from the gallery to the second level balcony. All spaces have high bands of continuous glass to provide uninterrupted private views to the many oak trees and natural landscaping.

Wilson House

Marlborough Sounds, New Zealand
John Daish Architects & Kebbell Daish

House area: 1780 square feet/165 square meters
Site area: 5 acres/2 hectares
Materials: timber frame with sonaguard exterior cladding

The opportunities in this project were presented by the extraordinary landscape: the bush, the sea, the steep hill, the views, the gathering of fresh water and the hinterland that lures wine enthusiasts from all over the world. This house is set on a ridge around a ground-level courtyard with an open bath, and two separate interiors hung off each side. A number of elements in the house are mixed up in the bath. Apart from the more than one tonne of hot, cold, creek and rainwater that fills it, the bath mixes the private and public lives of its inhabitants, the interior and exterior architecture, and individually framed views of the landscape and seascape. The densely organized plan is composed of eddy after eddy, as if the dynamics of water permeate the house at every level before the interior spills across the courtyard and into the bush.

Windy Hill

Northern Mississippi, USA
Ken Tate Architect

House area: 11,000 square feet/1022 square meters (including air conditioned part of pool house)
Site area: 2000 acres/809 hectares
Materials: exterior: antique Vermont weathering green roof slate, Texas limestone, antique heart pine timber, mahogany, leaded copper flashing, gutters, downspouts, and roof vents, Oklahoma flagstone, hand-forged iron gates and hinges, handmade brick pavers and detailing; interior: antique French limestone pavers with onyx cabochons, scored plaster and trompe l'oeil 'stone' walls, Portuguese handmade clay, antique heart pine, antique chestnut wood flooring, clay flooring, pine beams, limed paneled walls

Stretching for miles across the property, a gated private road winds from the edge of one of Mississippi's small towns. Turning onto the driveway beyond the big gates, prairie gives way to extensive gardens, and a Norman manor house is revealed. The house looks as old as the mountains. Indeed, its rough stonework, consists only of weathered rock, from the face of a mountain. Constructed over five years, the whole seems to have evolved over centuries, as did Norman residences on both sides of the English Channel.

Landscape architect René Fransen's plan drew Tate's architecture out into the countryside. Axes extend in all directions, punctuated by structures of Tate's design. Tate imbued the dovecote, pump houses, tractor shed, greenhouse, and poolhouse with the elegance that the French bring to the most utilitarian structures. The poolhouse terminates one end of the pool's axis, and faces the pool's arched and fountain-fed grotto. Ending the axis of the croquet lawn, a late renaissance exedra doubles as a garden seat, for gazing toward a newly created private lake. Off the rose garden, in what seems to be the dovecote, is the grandchildren's multi-story playhouse. Off its own cour d'honneur, the wood-paneled garage is but a preface to the wonders of the interiors beyond.

Inside, the Tates have marshaled their design teams in creating what at first seems to have grown by haphazard accretion, but then reveals itself to be an interior firmly grounded in classical ordering principles. Charme Tate contributed her own nuances to the process. In came flooring from a demolished chateau, and silk draperies hand-painted in London for the job. Antique tasseled passementerie adorns drapery surrounding a painted Portuguese bed. The longroom, breakfast room and stair hall have woodwork that was made in England, from re-milled antique heartwood. The woodwork's makers traveled to Mississippi, to install their paneling and niches, and to apply an authentic limed finish. Particularly brilliant among Ken Tate's moments here are things such as the box-bay, with its rough-hewn timbers and leaded glass windows, juxtaposed against the very formal French drawing room. Then, there is the brick-infilled half-timbering off one wing, and all the perfectly reproduced details that reveal the acute skill embodied in the Normans' joinery methods.

Wings

Escondido, California, USA
Norm Applebaum AIA, Architect

House area: 3200 square feet/297 square meters
Guest house area: 800 square feet/74 square meters
Site area: 2.5 acres/1 hectare
Materials: wood, steel, glass

It's dawn and as the sun rises above the horizon, the house begins to glisten. Like a bird ready for flight, it matches what nature offers as red-shouldered hawks glide below. Freedom is the word that describes this architecture. The edifice known as 'Wings' is owned by Richard C. Matheron, former United States Ambassador to Swaziland, Africa, and his wife Katherine. This Southern California contemporary home is pure design and reflects an open plan. It acknowledges the Japanese House and the principals of past great architects such as Shindler, Harris, Maybeck and Wright.

The architect was chosen because of his sensitivity to the environment, an element indispensable with regard to the Matherons' daily life in their new home. The home is a modern expression of sophisticated simplicity with visual extension of space achieved by use of dropped walls and floor-to-ceiling glass panels. The rhythmic fenestration fills the house with natural light in the daytime and the evening brings to the observer an illuminated roof line that appears to float above the clerestory glass. The materials used were expressed in an honest manner, 1x4 cedar siding lightly stained, exposed steel, painted oxide red primer, redwood and douglas fir with a clear oil finish, 3-score concrete masonry and a roof of corrugated steel panels painted with a copper emulsion paint.

This architect takes the California modern ideal of indoor-outdoor living in a highly individualized manner, believing that real architecture grows out of the land.

Wood Residence

Hillsborough, California, USA
House + House Architects
Brukoff Design Associates Inc.

House area: 4400 square feet/410 square meters
Site area: 0.75 acre/0.3 hectare
Materials: wood frame, cedar siding, redwood, stucco, cherry and maple wood, granite, slate, limestone, marble, stainless steel

In an affluent community south of San Francisco, this new home recedes into the center of its site, nestled into its south-facing slope. By a simple rotation, the house turns blank walls to the neighboring homes and opens wide to protected views. A detached three-car garage is connected to the house by a covered breezeway through a quiet garden with a sloping stone wall and a beautiful Japanese maple tree. A gray slate walkway leads to the front door past birch trees and a curving black steel fence. The crisp form of the house is achieved by the use of tightly spaced vertical wood siding and integrally colored stucco that layer the forms against one another in varying shades of taupe.

The living, dining, kitchen, study, powder and master suite are located on the main floor with wide expanses of glass to the views. Modulated ceiling shapes give definition and division between spaces that are open and flow together. Rooms spill out onto a large curving wood deck with glass panel railings that disappear against the view. At the lower floor, the family room, guest bedrooms, laundry and workshop are reached by a curving stairway with tall windows to a broad, protected view into the gardens.

The front door is fabricated in maple, cherry, ebony and stainless steel with flanking panels of sandblasted glass. A cylindrical cherry column frames the passage into the vaulted living/dining area where warm maple paneling on the ceiling glows. Cherry cabinetry and granite counters at the wet bar continue into the kitchen and in the powder room where they become sculpted art pieces. With windows on three sides, the kitchen and its adjacent seating area are bathed in natural light.

The Wood Residence was the recipient of the 2003 Custom Home Design Award.

Woods Drive Residence

Los Angeles, California, USA
Aleks Istanbullu Architects

House area: 6000 square feet/557 square meters
Materials: cherry wood, ochre plaster, marble counters, gold-leaf, glass railings, teak wood

The clients called for more contiguous living space in their home, while maintaining the exterior. The site is a hilltop with spectacular views of Los Angeles from downtown to the ocean. The existing house, built in the early 1990s, was essentially a 6800-square-foot (632-square-meter) white box with black windows.

The architect reorganized and renovated the interior of the home around the light and views at the site, and the need for a showplace for antiques and contemporary art. Some walls were removed, and the dining room ceiling was raised. The space was actually reduced for better

flow of space. A curved exterior wall transects the building, and leads one to the cherry wood front door. The interior portion of the curved wall has insets and niches to provide nooks for sculpture and other art. The wall is faced with ochre-colored acrylic plaster on one side, and teak paneling on the other.

The passage through the interior starts narrowly and then pans out to reveal the view. A broad living room is filled with fine antique furniture placed in conversational vignettes accented by antique Oriental rugs. A decorative wall with elaborate green damask upholstery and an ornate mirror provides a transition between the space for antiques and the rest of the contemporary interior.

Much of the first floor is organized around a two-story, light-filled central staircase court. Light from the stairway skylights and windows increases natural light throughout the home, particularly in the kitchen. The kitchen was completed, renovated, and faced in cherry wood with marble counters. Like the large living room, the bedroom is a broad expanse of open space punctuated by carefully chosen furniture. The large master bath sports marble counters and plenty of storage behind cherry cabinetry. A small vanity area was carved out of a niche between bathroom and closet.

Woollahra Residence

Woollahra, New South Wales, Australia
Alexander Tzannes Associates

House area: 5070 square feet/471 square meters
Site area: 6340 square feet/589 square meters
Materials: masonry structure, natural materials including various timber and stone finishes, zinc sheeting, mineral silicate paints to external render

The site comprised two terrace houses either side of a courtyard garden. Both terraces had been subject to numerous small alterations that left little original fabric intact. The single ownership of these properties presented an unexpected opportunity for this part of Sydney. The houses have been kept as separate buildings, one functioning as the primary house and the second as a guest house, the two connected only by the courtyard. The southern end of the courtyard is terminated with a loggia on the lower level, and a terrace off the main bedroom above.

The nature of the development is not apparent from the street. At the porch and in the entry there are glimpses to the garden, but only having descended the few steps to the living room is the full extent of the garden courtyard visible. All primary rooms are arranged around the courtyard garden. Each room has a different type of relationship to the garden, ranging from the limited glimpse available from a fixed projecting window in one corner of the entry, to the large, covered and framed concertina door openings from the living and dining rooms.

The elevation to the lane has been designed in high-quality robust materials. Facing the lane, the second level is housed within a zinc-clad roof which has narrow double-hung windows housed within the mansard shape to deliver light and cross ventilation. To the extent the configuration and orientation of the site allowed, principles of passive solar design have been employed. The varied degrees of enclosure, orientation and size of living spaces throughout allow for different levels of comfort in different spaces at all times of the day and year. Materials have been selected to provide the building with a high thermal mass. Protected openings allow doors and windows to be used in inclement weather.

Yellow Villa

Palanga, Lithuania
Vilius Ir Partneriai: Vilius Adomavicius and Vida Vysniauskiene

House area: 2960 square feet/275 square meters
Site area: 6674 square feet/620 square meters
Materials: brick, steel, glass, wood

The Yellow Villa is a house more typical of a resort town—a house for entertaining family and friends. Yellow was chosen as the major color, symbolizing youth, freedom and joy, reminiscent of summers at a seaside resort.

Along with the generous family accommodation, the guest rooms are spacious and welcoming, with bathrooms adjoining the double bedrooms. The house fuses east and west, with Lithuanian, European and Japanese influences. These influences include the Japanese-style roof structure, bright colors and abstract shapes and spaces. European influences are the Italian furniture and lighting designs, colorful French furniture and Danish armchairs, and German carpet with its Salvador Dali-like motifs. The Lithuanian influences are found in the clean lines of the architect-designed wardrobes, orange lampshades, and the futuristic, yellow bathroom. Modern Lithuanian artworks and ceramics, by the architects and local artists, decorate the house. The artistic is used to camouflage more functional aspects of the house—perforated tin is used on the sliding external fence; the sculptured handrail of the internal stair meshes with the circle sculpture at the top of the staircase, and the circular skylight above.

The house is a mixture of transparency and privacy. The many windows open up the house to the outside, just as the internal plan is open and transparent, while still maintaining a cosy atmosphere. However, privacy is guaranteed in this confined, urban site, while preserving views. These attributes have earned the house the distinction amongst the local residents as 'the most beautiful in Palanga.'

Index